PLAGUES and PLACEBOS

Part I

Published by:

FriesenPress

Suite 300 – 852 Fort Street
Victoria, BC, Canada V8W 1H8

www.friesenpress.com

Distributed to the trade by The Ingram Book Company

For MOTHER

"My Mother had a great deal of trouble with me, but I think she enjoyed it." - Mark Twain

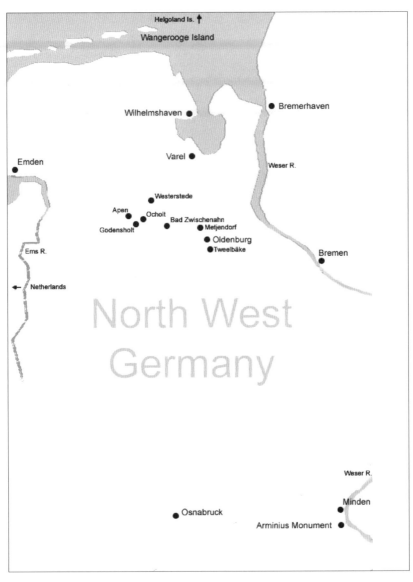

Helgoland Is.

Wangerooge Island

Bremerhaven

Wilhelmshaven

Varel

Emden

Weser R.

Westerstede

Apen

Ocholt

Bad Zwischenahn

Godensholt

Metjendorf

Oldenburg

Ems R.

Tweelbäke

Bremen

Netherlands

North West Germany

Weser R.

Minden

Osnabruck

Arminius Monument

This compressed map of Lower Saxony introduces the places of my childhood, both before and during the Hitler era, as the names appear in the following chapters.

Chapter 1

It was a sunny day, June 23, 1920, with magnolia blooming, robins singing, and bees buzzing, when a young woman, highly pregnant and in labour contractions, arrived at the door of the Waisen Haus, an orphanage in Varel, a small town in north west Germany. Paraphrasing Charles Dickens, it was the best of times weather-wise for the advent of her first-born, however, for the future of the child and for the country, it was the worst of times, the age of darkness, the season of despair. Starting the war, Germany had wiped her good name off the map within a few years. In far-away Paris, the nation's uncertain destiny had just been decided upon at the Peace Conference on the Quay d'Orsay. World leaders from twenty-five enemy powers, including the British prime minister, the president of the United States, the French premier, and the prime minister of Italy, had wrapped up their talks and signed treaties forcing Germany to accept the terms of harsh reparations as a consequence of the Great War the generals had started in 1914.

Why would a young mother-to-be, about to give birth, have sought out the local Waisen Haus under such circumstances? Did she, in desperation, want to die there, providing her newborn with the means to claim orphan status? Not likely, for if *in extremis* she would have been taken to a hospital to be delivered. Was she a single orphan herself, of child-bearing age, pregnant, about to give birth? Highly unlikely; the young woman had married well and was not eligible for admission to such an institution. Admittedly, the situation in Germany under the first democratic government, the Weimar Republic, was unstable.

The brutal nature of the Great War had totally altered the human perspective on the morality of such slaughters. Resigned into an insecure future, the young men who had returned home from the trenches of the western front, after risking their lives for Kaiser and Fatherland, were attempting to make up for lost time, to re-establish themselves in families and careers. The father of the unborn child that the woman was carrying had himself been a victim, critically wounded in the fighting. He had survived and, although barely coping with a severe disability, been able to find employment in his profession as a schoolteacher. Although the Treaty of Versailles caused a great deal of resentment and economic hardship, teachers in Germany are civil servants; the father's secure position would rule out the need to seek the support of a public institution for their child to be born.

I have always enjoyed the irony of my quasi-mythic birth; however, the details are prosaic. Put simply, at the time of my primal scream, my grandfather was the administrator of the Varel Waisen Haus. I was born legitimately to married parents and do not solicit compassion for the circumstances surrounding my arrival. All was quite proper, promising and propitious, and the midwife was paid promptly. My mother, while visiting her in-laws, had just climbed the local water tower, a newly-constructed landmark, executed in contemporary *art nouveau* style, a public works project, designed to create employment for returned soldiers. It may or may not have been the exertion of climbing the three hundred or so steps, but when my mother-to-be got to the top, labour did start there and then. Her gestational clock had run out, and there was no time to return to their modest teacher's residence in the small village of Godensholt for the blessed event. It was her in-laws' master bedroom in a centuries-old building, the orphanage in Varel, which would bear witness to her birthing throes.

While the wrought-iron inscription above the Baroque Waisen Haus portal attests to the founder's covenant with his God, the door lintel displays a rider to the contract, "*Dominus protectat,*" May the Lord Protect.

Not only was I born in an orphanage; my birthplace is also a building designated as a national historic site. This distinction is not the result of my birth; nor is it of recent origin, the edifice having obtained status as a monument a hundred years before. The exterior alone is significant; its portal bears ornate, foot-high letters of wrought iron that attest to its endowment by Count Anton Günther in the seventeenth century. The Latin inscription *QUID RETRIBUAM DOMINO A.D. 1671* pleads the Count's commitment to a covenant with God in the billboard fashion of his time and proclaims his part of the deal to finance the erection of this harbour of refuge. The door lintel bears the inscription *DOMINUS PROTECTAT* as an appendix, a rider to an insurance contract, urging the Almighty to keep an eye on things. To this day, the building, executed in bright red bricks, the material at hand, remains in remarkable condition.

At the time when I was born under its tiled roof, the Waisen Haus was a going concern, with my grandfather in charge of twenty-four homeless boys and girls

My paternal grandfather Heinrich Asche, my "Opa," was originally a tradesman. Although his fame never measured up to that of the shoemaker Hans Sachs who lived three hundred years before him, my Opa was also a cobbler. While that fifteenth-century poet (later immortalized in Richard Wagner's musical drama *Die Meistersinger*) had the time and means to write verses and rhymes, by Opa's time, the Industrial Revolution had deluged the market with cheaper footwear and put an end to shoemaking as a sophisticated and lucrative trade. Heinrich Asche changed careers, becoming the steward of the local poorhouse and orphanage, continuing with leather tanning on the side. From the village of Tweelbäke, he worked his way up to the position of majordomo, the administrator, of the more distinguished Waisen Haus in Varel, where he remained until he died in the early 1920s.

A nineteenth century Ambrotype photograph, taken of my grandmother on her wedding-day.

The Heinrich Asche Family

Although the orphan children in Opa's care went barefoot in summer and used wooden clogs in winter, they had good shoes to wear to church on Sundays. For any repairs or new soles, well, they were in the right place. Even Opa's young son Adolf, a graduate of the Oldenburg Teachers' College, had learned the cobbler's trade and applied it for years to keep his own family's feet in good fettle. It was Adolf who, upon his return from the western front, had courted and married Amalie, one of the Schütte girls from a Methodist family who had been good neighbours when the Asches lived in Tweelbäke. Amalie, highly pregnant, was climbing the steps of the water tower while visiting her in-laws and gave birth in their bedroom.

For my parents' wedding, the Schüttes insisted on a Methodist rather than a Lutheran pastor.

Mother, Amalie Schütte Asche, freshly married and full of expectation for a successful life at the side of her husband, unaware of the adversities the future held for her.

The orphanage's working manager Georg Meier was on military leave of absence, to supervise the boys, in their long working pants and barefoot, bringing in the 1917 potato crop.

Adolf Asche, successful graduate, fresh from the Oldenburg Teachers' College.

In 1999, when the approaching millennium inspired a renovation and facelift of the historic building, the work crew discovered a cookie tin above the wooden ceiling of the Waisen Haus kitchen, a 1902 time capsule, in which Heinrich Asche, later my "Opa," had left a handwritten, punctilious account of the operation. In that year, the Varel Waisen Haus employed a permanent staff of three. Georg Meier was the working manager for a salary of 300 marks per annum, plus one sheep with lambs. Fritz Janssen worked as a labourer, at 2.25 marks daily plus board and a room, and Marie Dierks, head maid, received an annual salary of 200 marks. None of them had to pay income tax at that time. A male and a female tailor were under contract, and four Varel merchants competed for the supply of goods. The number of dependent wards varied between twenty and thirty. (At the time of my birth, the Waisen Haus accommodated twenty-four children, seventeen boys and seven girls.) The institution received no subsidies; it was a self-sustaining operation of some thirty cows, twenty pigs, five sheep and lambs, thirty chickens, and twelve turkeys. To keep horses was uneconomical because their meat was excluded from human consumption. The day before, Heinrich Asche had sold a 1407-pound ox at the price of 464.31 marks, at thirty-three pfennigs a pound. The orphanage's 1902 operating costs of 12,572.27 marks compare favourably with the returns of 12,818.18 marks, coming out on top of the heap by a surplus of 245.41 marks.

It took a hundred years to uncover a cookie tin, a 1902 time capsule, stored above the orphanage's kitchen ceiling.

For its time, one hundred and ten years ago, the orphanage was a business of some substance. The institution operated under the supervision of a board of four trustees, consisting of the mayor of Varel, a government assessor, the local Member of the Legislative Assembly, and a Pastor Graap, with whom Opa Asche often did not see eye to eye. It was the pastor's contention that the children should come for their catechism lectures to the pastorage, a building adjacent to the church and very cold in the winter, whereas the task seemed simpler, better supervised, and warmer in the spacious Waisen Haus kitchen with large tables for writing and long benches to seat thirty. Keeping the students at home would save the labour of dressing the girls properly and having them safely conducted into town and back. In the end, they reached a compromise that enhanced the pastor's visits by a large meal, a glass of wine, and a cigar from my Opa's humidor. There is no mention of Heinrich Asche's own salary; it must have satisfied the daily needs and generated the funds to send his son to the teachers' college in Oldenburg.

When I turned two and Mother was occupied with her second pregnancy, which resulted in the birth of Werner, the first of my two brothers, I was "farmed out" to my grandparents in Varel. One day, Oma and Father's unmarried sister, Tante Ida, took me across the inner court to the orphanage's laundry kitchen containing two enameled iron bathtubs and a large, peat-fired laundry kettle. I remember getting undressed and splashing contentedly in the warm water. Tante Ida also undressed, presumably to bathe in the other tub. In my infant ignorance, I was astounded, seeing the authority of my aunt, naked, standing next to my tub. I could not take my eyes off her hairy pubic triangle, which appeared level with my face. Oma Asche noted my staring and told Tante Ida to cover herself. Tante Ida's manner dumbfounded me for the rest of my life. Was her motive expediency, to get into her bathtub which stood against the other wall? Was it female exhibitionism, inadvertent carelessness, or plain indifference? Did she want to see the reaction of a little boy or just to revel in the spinster's unfulfilled dream of cuddling a small child in her lap in the warm water? She might have joined me, had her mother not interfered.

Gerd Asche, circa 1922. It was uncommon to distinguish the gender of small children by their clothing; this fancy kirtle was *haute couture* for both boys and girls.

My Opa Asche was a nature and health fanatic. He used to do his morning wash at a pond in the garden, well protected against spectators by tall rushes. When he died at the age of seventy-two, I remember Father arriving on his bicycle from Godensholt, taking me to the Vareler Busch, a park, to pick a bunch of wild anemones to place into Grandfather's folded hands while he was lying in the casket. My Opa was the first dead person I saw. The doctor said it was stomach cancer, and that diagnosis, without an autopsy, was accepted by the family. In retrospect, however, the clinical picture resembles the fulminating course of pancreatic cancer, more so since that affliction recently took Kurt, the younger of my two brothers. His medical history, corroborating the disease's heritability, resembles that of his grandfather. Opa's funeral itself did not affect or impress me. At least not as much as my vision of Tante Ida.

Gerd and his little brother Kurt under the watchful eyes of Oma and Opa Asche by his beloved garden pond.

In May of 1919, my father had accepted the position of head schoolmaster to the two-classroom school in Godensholt, a small remote village in rural Lower Saxony where I spent the first years of my life. When I was three, the American dollar equaled four million marks. A new currency, the renten mark, replacing the reichs mark, was established and became valuable. The first reaction to good money came to our small village as an Electrolux salesman. Rural electricity had just arrived, and to demonstrate the quality of his product, he dropped a new groschen coin (ten pfennigs) on the carpet which he ostentatiously allowed his machine to suck up under the pretence of demonstrating the power of the vacuum. He then allowed me to search for the coin in the dust receptacle bag and it was mine to keep. This small present placed a certain burden of obligation on my parents who had watched. Mother had always dreamed of owning a vacuum cleaner; they bought the appliance, complete with skids, and it served our family for decades.

Father, Adolf Asche, appointed to headmaster of the two-classroom Godensholt School.

Even in the small village of Godensholt, money lost its value rapidly. In 1923, with inflation, this amount would buy a loaf of dark rye bread.

Buying goods on installments was in the future; you either paid the full amount or had to do without. Their next purchase staggers belief--a new Ibach upright piano, which they could afford by saving the extra disability pension Father received for the loss of his leg for the Fatherland--blood and tears for Bach, Brahms, and Debussy.

The easy money coming my way through the calculated generosity of the vacuum cleaner salesman I spent on candy, called bonbons. My monetary success seemed to thrive when I discovered a fifty-pfennig piece that Mother had placed on top of the dresser for safe keeping. Encouraged by my previous experience, I promptly took the money to Meins' grocery store and turned it into a treasure of sweet divinity. Later that day, I heard Father coming from classes and my guilt (I knew, this was a severe misdeneanor) made me hide in the bushes behind the house. He called, and I had to answer, begging not to be punished. He gave me a lecture that the offence was so serious, having hurdled the inflation, that he could not think of any punishment to fit that transgression. I went scot-free. I did not feel terribly guilty and was relieved that there would be no tar-and-feathering.

The currency reform that brought us the Swedish vacuum cleaner attracted other pedlars from abroad. Because of the proximity to Holland, we received regular visits from a cheese seller who carried his wheels of Gouda or the balls of sweeter Edamer, with or without caraway seeds, on his bicycle, and Mother usually was his customer. The Holländer held his stock in a basket-like baggage carrier over the front wheel, distinguishing him from the locals; our German bikes came with a flat carrier over the rear wheel. The trader explained the advantage--he would more easily notice if a red ball of Edamer cheese were to roll off--and we agreed. To us, the bike's unorthodox construction was assurance of the merchandise's genuine "Holländische" provenance.

My playmates in Godensholt were Erna and Sofie, both a little older. During play I had picked a bunch, an *umbel*, of *Hollunder Beeren*, black elderberries, *sambucus nigra*, also known as *Flieder Beeren*. The ripe fruit seductively reminded me of delicious black currants. However, they taste awful, and I had to spit them out. Father had made a whistle for me out of the plant's hollow stem, and that had attracted me to the *Hollunder.*

(Elderberries are said to be endowed with medicinal powers but they taste too awful to put to the test.

Our adventures took Erna, Sofie, and me to their barn, into a comfortable cubicle of fresh straw, inviting more secluded play. Although the girls may have been five or six, the nature of our activity was more exploratory; none of us had reached that critical age of gender consciousness. The intimate play in the straw did not sexually excite me (I may have been unreceptive at that age) but the incident remains in my memory as something unusual. It was probably not "playing doctor," as none of us had ever been to one, but plain natural curiosity on the part of Erna and Sofie. They were fascinated by the difference, with the urge to touch and feel my appendage with its mysterious change in consistency. When they insisted on reciprocating by self-exposure, I was at a loss and felt embarrassed; where I had more, they had less. In a pinch, the bunch of berries still in my hand, ceremoniously, as if dispensing sacramental offerings, I inserted each girl with one of my little black elderberries.

Our plays, however, were not all cream and honey. On another day I had a disagreement with Erna and came home with my face badly scratched up. I remember Father getting very angry but I don't know if there were any representations to the family who lived next door. Erna's folks had a garden with translucent "August" apples. Her father was blind and received a war pension. Erna had two nice brothers, Arthur and Emil. Arthur phoned me in later years but I never met them again face-to-face. Erna married and moved to Keyhausen, a place near Zwischenahn; occasionally, I think of the girl and our mutual experiences as playmates, and I wonder, if she would remember them.

A traumatic incident happened one afternoon while I was in the hall of our residence. The main door, fitted with a framed window above to admit light, had not been inspected since before the war. Suddenly, a gust of wind pushed the entire casement inward and it came crashing down, breaking into pieces, the shards barely missing me. I could only stammer "Fa . . ., Fa . . . ." Then Father came and reassured me. However, the memory of the near miss has not faded over the past eighty-five years.

On another occasion, an injury caused my parents' concern. During my curious explorations, I climbed up a plank or door which was leaning against a fence between two buildings. I made it up all the way with the result that the door became top-heavy and flipped. I came down on the other side of the fence with a nasty head laceration. Father took me to a doctor in Oldenburg, hiring a horse-drawn light wagon, a *Federwagen*, to take us to the train station at Ocholt. I remember becoming angry at the doctor for hurting me but I don't think the cut was serious, and I felt so much better, that on the way home I was allowed to sit on the front bench next to the driver. To reach Godensholt before dark, he had brought the horse to a gentle trot. From my privileged view, I witnessed an unusual display: unexpectedly, while running, before my eyes, the horse raised its tail, an opening below it became large, and the horse began to evacuate while engaged in the labour of pulling our wagon. I felt not embar-rassment but empathy with the poor mare who had given no sign of intention nor would she have been allowed to stop for the procedure that I could not imagine being performed without rest and quiet. But this was rural life, and nobody cared about the creature's need to take a break even for a vital function.

It is said that burns in children occur more frequently when there is instability in the family, but my injury, I think, must have been a true accident. I vaguely associate a life-long burn to the inside of my right forearm with Mother's cooking jam on the stove. I never thought of asking her about it. When I had the measles and, I believe, also the mumps, I did not suffer, and my parents took good care of me.

One day, when I was five, I woke up in the morning and saw something sparkling and shiny new on wheels standing next to my bed. Then my parents came. The bicycle was my birthday present; I was anxious to ride it. In front of the school where we lived stood an oak tree, the *Friedens Eiche*, the Peace Oak, a memento of the 1871 Peace of Versailles, planted by people who were glad the slaughter of the Franco-Prussian War was over. It was around this fenced-in living peace memorial where I learned to ride the bike. The thrill of successfully mounting it by myself and the elation of balancing were a feeling I had again later in my life, landing successfully after my first solo flight.

The Godensholt Peace Oak in front of the school, our residence, a symbol of my early childhood trials, failures, and final triumph in circumnavigating its fence on my bike.

Father's two-classroom school included the principal's residence. My bedroom was next to the school's entrance hall;

in the morning at eight, the rumble of the students coming in woke me up. Through the wall, I could hear their wooden shoes clopping on the concrete floor. Then the time came for my own enrolment into the first class. At the request of the district medical officer, Mother took me to the preschool examination. Together with about a dozen other little candidates, we boys were undressed completely and, stark naked, ran around the room in unbound, atavistic freedom. This would not have drawn my attention had not a few of them shown an erection of their little penises that stuck out like thin pencils. I later wondered why some displayed this reaction and others showed no affect. Were these children in their mind equating nakedness with sexual arousal? Had they perhaps even been subject to experiences at their young age in their own family? I do not know the doctor's motives for his insensitive request to undress all boys. He may have been a demobilized military medical officer spurning the labour of private practice and making his work as a government official short and efficient. I doubt, though, that his time-saving batching would allow the discovery of a congenitally dislocated hip, an undescended testicle, a hernia, an enlarged spleen, a defective heart valve, or a contagious disease such as tuberculosis, unless by individual and more detailed scrutiny. He would submit his fee for the examination of some twelve school children and be home in time for supper.

Times have changed; a modern-day pediatrician would have noted that none of the boys was circumcised. Loss of one's foreskin would have been considered a mutilation and would have raised speculations even before the Nazi era. A *Beschneidung,* a circumcision, I could see only on religious paintings of the Old Masters that I found in Father's art magazines. The pictures claimed to show the circumcision of the infant Jesus. No one knew what took place, and the paintings did not reveal details of the procedure.

During the first school years in Godensholt, my conversation with the other kids was in *Platt Deutsch*, Low German.

Gerd Asche

For instance, we called Saturday, the highlight of the week without school or catechism, "*Saterdag.*" Low German was considered inferior to the sophisticated *Hoch Deutsch*, the language claiming two other names for that significant sixth day. Called "*Samstag*" in the south of Germany, and "*Sonnabend*" (sun evening) in the north, the latter name was introduced by the English-born St. Boniface, apostle of the Germans, in the eighth century. The word "*Sonnabend*" has greater appeal to me; it denotes the promise of sunny weather, and joyful anticipation similar to Holy Eve, New Year's Eve, and Easter Eve.

One idiosyncrasy of High German is apparent in the pronunciation of the letter "s." If it precedes a "t" or a "p," sophisticated Germans pronounce it as "sh." For example, "stein," stone, becomes "*shtein*"; the word "respect" is spoken as "*reshpect,*" and "*springen,*" to jump, becomes "*shpringen.*" Another distinction from rural people was the pronunciation of the letter "r." In the country, it is tongue-rolled, similar to the Scottish and some Bavarian dialects, whereas the city people who consider themselves perhaps more erudite, pronounce it in a stylized, throaty French fashion, a legacy retained from Napoleon's occupation.

A class photograph taken during my second year of school, with our teacher, Herr Osterloh supervising, prompted our commenting and joking about the placement of our hands. Some boys, when in the sitting position, had placed their hands, quite naturally, in their laps, but even at that age this position seemed to have sexual connotations. These controversies were innocent banter among children of a rural population with close contact to farm animals and their reproduction as part of a natural world. When the prints came out I felt relieved to see that I had my right hand draped across my neighbour's shoulder and my left resting on the thigh at just the critical moment.

1925 class in Godensholt. Seating in alphabetical order placed me to the far right, row one, next to the teacher, Herr Osterloh. My two playmates, Erna and Sofie, are seated at the extreme left, arms interlocked.

One boy of our class was absent on the day that photograph was taken. Johann Tammen, about my age, whose family lived in our neighbourhood, was a tall and very skinny boy, with whom we had very little contact. He often missed classes because he was ill. In an old photograph of the Tammen family, taken on a day they had invited us, their neighbours, to an outing in a horse-drawn spring wagon, Johann appears obviously impaired physically, too tall and lanky for his age. Seen with a physician's eyes, his disability seems to have been a connective tissue disease such as Marfan Syndrome. His immune-compromised condition would also explain his contracting the deadly infantile paralysis. One day, unexpectedly, Mother told me that Johann had died suddenly from *Kinder Lähmung*, children's lameness, infantile paralysis, now better known as polio. For a small village, the death of a child was a major event. Our class prepared for the funeral; Herr Osterloh taught us to sing a chorale that left me with a profound impression about this Jesus, a real leader who would show us the way in our life. The hymn, composed during the miserly Protestant Revolution of the Thirty Years War, was austere but consoling. Both its simple melody and reassuring words gripped me profoundly. I believe I cried during the singing, not so much over the loss of Johann but rather from the effect this beautiful song of "*Jesus geh' voran*" had on me on such a sad occasion.

Jesus, still lead on,
'Til our rest be won!
And, although the way be cheerless,
We will follow, calm and fearless;
Guide us by Thy hand
To our Fatherland.
If the way be drear,
If the foe be near,
Let not faithless fears o'ertake us,
Let not faith and hope forsake us,
For, through many a foe,
To our home we go.

We buried our classmate in the small Godensholt cemetery. Soon after, Father accepted a position in Metjendorf; our family moved, and other events took my attention until many years later when the death of young Johann Tammen and the simple melody would intrude on my mind again during the days when I worked as a medical intern among rows of humming iron lungs during the polio epidemic in Winnipeg, Canada.

To a child, rural life did have its advantages over living in the city. We ran barefoot in the summer to save on shoes. There was no contamination with glass shards or nails. Bottles or jars were recycled and bent nails straightened. On hot summer days, our parents biked us to the "*Drakamp*," a small shallow lake. I was fascinated when I discovered in the reeds a mysterious decoy hut with pillows and blankets to comfort the Nimrods stalking for game fowl.

The Drakamp Lake was secluded, and we boys bathed without trunks. My parents also took me to the Godensholter "*Tief*" (deep), a small winding river, the course of which was corrected and straightened later. The water was deep enough, reaching to his chest, for Father to keep his balance on his one leg. I remember him cradling me in his arms and holding me in the water; it was not unpleasant but I think its coolness made me gasp.

Father's war injury was a severe handicap. A piece of French shrapnel had shattered his left leg; at first, it was amputated below the knee, leaving him with the loss of a lower limb, a disability relatively easy to overcome since the important functions of the knee joint are preserved. Unfortunately, the portion of skin behind the knee, which the surgeon used as a flap to cover and pad the bone stump for later prosthesis weight-bearing, did not "take"; it became gangrenous and infected the knee joint. Thus, Father ended up with a much more traumatic and more impairing amputation. To obtain a sufficient full-thickness skin cover, the surgeon had to sacrifice the entire knee. Father needed a compound prosthesis that was held in place by a wide shoulder strap. During his rehabilitation, a military orderly had been assigned as his support. At night, after he had gone to bed, the artificial leg, of light-brown skin-coloured leather, with chromium-plated metal joints, sock and shoe still attached, was standing grotesquely, disembodied, in the corner of the bedroom; to me it appeared as a part of Father.

Recovering from the full-length leg amputation, discharged from the hospital, Father and his previous comrade-in-arms have made friends with three barefoot urchins. The strap over Father's right shoulder is holding the left-sided leg prosthesis in place.

Gerd Asche

Despite the loss of one leg, Father had retrained himself to ride the bike, using a two-wheeler with its pedals rigidly geared to the rear wheel so that pushing the bike would automatically rotate the toothed pedal wheel. This was done out of necessity. Unlike a toy steam engine that is kept going by a flywheel, the initial pedal push had to furnish the rider and his bike with enough momentum to complete the full rotation for the good leg's next application of downward push. The inane prosthesis was only dead weight, unable to push the pedal down. To get rolling and to maintain balance, his only live leg had to give the vehicle enough impulse to turn the pedal wheel full circle for the next opportunity to apply power. Although a clip-on attachment to pull up the pedal would have enabled him to compensate for the lack of push on the other pedal, he had to have his only leg ready for an emergency, should he lose balance and need to stop, and if the leg were fastened to the pedal, a sudden stop would be disastrous.

As a teacher, Father was progressive and had some original ideas about teaching aids, one of which may appear a mere banality but received enthusiastic approval from his colleagues. I remember that he prepared and introduced at the teachers' conference in Oldenburg an outline of the Land Oldenburg, punched and cut out carefully from heavy, grey cardboard. The students could use this template for the study of local geography by placing and outlining it on their slates. He was quite interested in gardening and planted a lot of fruit trees behind the Godensholt school. Years later I saw how they had grown and were bearing beautiful apples. I preferred the flavour of *Cox's Orange* over the slightly sour taste of the thick-skinned *Schöner von Boskop*.

As a father, Dad must have been anxious to take me, his oldest, out for a bike tour once I had become proficient. When I was six, we cycled to the Weser Gebirge Mountains, the Porta Westfalica near Minden, the site of the German victory over the Roman general Quintilius Varus and his army in A.D. 9. A statue overlooking the Weser River valley depicts the

German leader Arminius raising his sword. Father, wearing his prosthesis, had bicycled more than two hundred kilometres; it took us two days to get there. Using the artificial leg, he walked and pushed the bike up the mountain to the imposing monument. His leg stump must have been painful, however, he wanted to dedicate our journey to my historical and patriotic education, a war-wounded father's pilgrimage to a national shrine. To rest his leg, we sat on the steps of the giant memorial where he told me about the dramatic events of nearly two thousand years before.

The Arminius monument, destination of our bicycle journey when I was six.

Three Roman legions, the 17th, 18th, and 19th, altogether about 15,000 men, were returning from the conquest of the land between the Rhine and the Elbe Rivers, about the area of our present Lower Saxony. The German Arminius, according to Martin Luther bearing the German name Hermann, "Leader of the Army," had lured the Roman General Varus to take a route set up for an ambush, through a narrows that forced their unassailable battle formations to break into a defenceless thin line that would stretch over miles. When the column was halfway through, the Germans attacked, raining down spears and arrows, and then, with the Romans in disarray, descended on them with swords and knives. Within hours, more than 10,000 Roman soldiers lay dying or dead while the survivors fought their way back to the Rhine. In Rome, Caesar

Augustus banged his fists against the palace door, shouting: "Quintilius Varus, give me back my legions!" Following this ignominy, the numbers 17, 18, and 19 were excluded from naming legions. "The Rhine was firmly established as the eastern limit of Roman expansion and," Father explained, "for hundreds of years, northern Germany and Scandinavia remained free from the influence of Roman culture, law, and domination." He was unaware how a few short years later the history textbooks of Goebbels' Nazi Ministry of Culture and Enlightenment would twist the historical interpretation.

Father was very musical and socially oriented. Other schoolteachers came on their bicycles from Apen and surrounding towns, the bulky violin-cello cases strapped to the back, for an evening of piano and string music at our house. I best remember Mozart's sparkling happy-sounding Minuet from the E-major Symphony and learned to play it myself. Father had a stuffed owl, Greek icon of wisdom, mounted and standing on top of the Ibach piano. His favourite pieces were Beethoven's Bagatelles and the charming Minuet in G by Paderewski, the same Paderewski who, as the Polish prime minister, had been a ratifier of the Versailles Peace Treaty. When Father played the *fortissimo* parts, the piano, and with it the owl, went into harmonic resonance, causing the stuffed animal to sway and nod back and forth as though in rhythm with the musical fare. Mother loved to sing from Handel's Messiah: "I know that my redeemer liveth" and the *Largo* from his Xerxes opera, accompanied by Father on the piano.

As a teacher during music lessons, Father used the viola (Bratsche), and we kept the instrument after his death until we moved to Oldenburg, at first to the Bremer Chaussee (a Napoleonic, German-adopted French name for highway) No. 37 and then to the Bremer Strasse No. 27. Somehow, H. H., my classmate and a musician's son (his father was conductor of the theatre orchestra), learned of this instrument in our possession and asked if he could borrow it. Mother, who was very astute in many things, became aware that when the instrument was returned, it was no longer a Bratsche but an ordinary violin. We have kept quiet and written off the loss of the more valuable instrument as our contribution to the growth and development of the local music world. In the meantime, H. H. has passed on. I used to admire his talents and was for a short time a member of his quartet presenting his sweet naïve little German songs such as:

You and I, by moonlight,
Alone on a little bench
Boy, oh boy, that would be wonderful,
But not quite without risk . . .
Du und ich, im Mondenschein,
auf einer kleinen Bank allein.
Junge, Junge, das wär' herlich,
aber nicht ganz ungefaehrlich . . .
Another, which I remember well, was:
Just for you
have I taken English lessons privately
just for you.
From my Sunday suit I had the spots removed,
Just for you.
Anything I would do.
Bring every sacrifice,
just for you
anything, anything, out of love for you.
da da dah
Ihnen zuliebe hab'ich heimlich Englisch gelernt,
Ihnen zuliebe.
Aus meinem Sonntagsanzug sind die Flecken entfernt,
Ihnen zuliebe.
Alles, hätt' ich gemacht,
jedes Opfer gebracht,
Ihnen zuliebe,
alles, alles Ihnen zuliebe,
da da da

During Father's Godensholt musical *soirees*, for refreshments, Mother used to serve a *"Bowle,"* a punch, usually made with wine, homemade, of course, and peaches or strawberries, spiced with the lemon-flavoured elderberry blossoms floating on top. Everyone had a good time while in Godensholt. One of Father's best friends was Carl B., a fellow teacher and acquaintance from their days at the Teachers' Academy in Oldenburg. Carl had, I believe, a higher position as a teacher in a Mittel Schule. He had a fine house in Westerstede and two boys, the oldest one named Enno. Father took many photos while visiting the B.s in Westerstede, one depicting six boys and a little girl, my cousin Eleanor, lined up in a row.

Seven friends met and played in the garden of father's teacher friend.

After we had moved to Metjendorf, the B.s returned the visit. After lunch, I took Enno and his cousin Viktor, both of the same age, to the Metjendorfer Heide, a deserted heath, later the site of a large military airport. At that time, the place was wild and desolate, and I remember the two boys trying to introduce me into self-gratification. They said: "If you rub long enough, it will feel good." I tried and rubbed but did not at that time reach any satisfaction. I realize now that to succeed, there must be an erection first, which I did not achieve. I may

not have been mature or receptive enough and had no previous contact or stimulation by any sexual exposure. There
was no furtive slyness or intimation of homosexuality about
the way the friends introduced me. I assume that one of them
came upon the resulting orgasm by experimentation and
passed the discovery on to his friend, and they wanted me to
share and enjoy the pleasure of the novelty.

Once, exploring Father's night drawer, I found an unusual
thing, a soft translucent, ring-shaped rubber object that struck
me as something secretive and intimate, but I did not know
what to do with it. I may have been about ten; I played with
it but did not have the presence of mind to unroll it or inflate
it to a balloon. I simply had no idea how or where to apply it.
At my age, I was unaware of the need to control pregnancy
and the devastating impact an additional child would have on
a family during the era of economic depression and salary
reduction. The unrecognized condom was the extent of my
pre-sexual experiences until I was at least fourteen and had
less sophisticated encounters in the Hitler Jugend. I did,
however, not face the type of molestation or homosexuality
which seems to be common nowadays. The reason probably
was the notoriety assigned to the homosexual activity of a
prominent Nazi, Ernst Roehm, who was said to have been
hanged for his alternate preference. A law, introduced by the
Nazis under Paragraph 175, made homosexuality, together
with religious sects and cults such as the "*Bibel Forschers*"
(Bible Pushers), a crime, punishable by imprisonment or
confinement to a concentration camp. During my later school
days at the Gymnasium in Oldenburg, we, amongst ourselves, made jesting derogatory references to the "175ers."

There was very little alcohol around in these times;
Schnapps and beer were looked down on. Father made
wine. Since grapes were a luxury he could not afford, he
used apples to make not cider but properly fermented and
decanted wine. I do not remember him drinking beer. Mother
said that he was inebriated once, weaving his bike on the

road from left to right. It cannot have been bad, for there is no record of any fall, even for a one-legged handicapped rider. The lights on our bikes were carbide lanterns. We placed the crystals, lumps of grey rocks, into the bottom container, added water to a small tank on top, and opened a valve; the water dropped into the carbide chamber where the two elements formed acetylene gas. I remember the light being quite bright, but by the time we moved away, these lamps had been replaced by the electric generators coupled to the bike wheel which only give light when the bike is in motion. The carbide lanterns, I imagine, were liable to explode. The light generated was excellent and all bikes came with brackets for carbide lamps.

A different type of magic lantern came to Godensholt in the form of a film projector. Father allowed me to go along with the older schoolchildren to watch the show in the hall at Meins' store and Guest House. The black and white film was without sound and badly scratched, and these shortcomings enhanced the impression of the film's horrors of the recent war, the soldiers emerging from the trenches, running, and abruptly falling down, dead. All movements were abrupt, much too fast, and grotesque. It may have been an early propaganda effort by the government of the Weimar Republic, struggling to stay in power against the rising militant right-wing Nazi party. If this was indeed their goal, their efforts proved to be in vain.

Another failed measure, also a reaction to the war and the heavy reparations payments imposed by the Versailles Treaty, was the government attempt to economize by combining religious and secular education under one roof of the Ministry of Churches and Schools. Pastors of the two official religions, Lutheran and Roman Catholic, were, like the teachers, salaried civil servants. While the school curriculum was supervised by the *Schulrat*, a school inspector, the obligatory subject of religious education was to be guided by the local clergy. However, as Godensholt did not have a church or a pastor, religious instruction fell under the authority of the pastor in the neighbouring town of Apen who openly castigated the poor state of spiritual instruction in Godensholt. It seemed like a repetition of the controversy between Pastor Graap and my Opa in Varel. Church was pitted against secular authority, and my dad would have none of it. His teaching methods were none of the Apen pastor's business. "We will follow, calm and fearless" was not Father's way. Instead, he ignored the reproves from the man of the cloth, and that included ignoring his Sunday services. We did not go to church except when we visited the town of Oldenburg where Mother insisted that we attend the services of her Methodist congregation. That personal schism between the pastor and my grandfather in charge of the orphanage, carried over to my father, the schoolteacher, explains my deficiency in religious education.

My birth had coincided with the time immediately following World War I, when the Zeitgeist, the spirit of the time, was one of defeat, of the need to recover from the debacle, and to put aside the former arrogant German imperious attitude. Little did Germans realize how soon a more aggressive nationalism would resurface; many had naively forgotten the lesson of the recent war and seemed to receive the Nazis with open arms.

The *Friedens Eiche*, the Peace Oak, planted at the end of the Franco-Prussian war, before World War I, the tree around which I learned to ride my bicycle, had stood in front of the school for several generations. Many years later, after World War II and at the conclusion of my medical studies, I visited Godensholt again, looking for the tree that had played such an important role in my early days. The village had been under attack by Canadian troops; all public buildings were left intact. However, of the *Friedens Eiche*, symbol of my childhood and of my national feelings, only a stump remained. The majestic oak was gone. I learned that not the victorious allies but German Nazis had chopped it down during the last days of their rule. The fanatics wanted no reminder of the shameful Versailles Treaty; they saw peace as defeatism and cowardice.

Chapter 2

Father had applied for the position of school principal in a location nearer to Oldenburg, a major education centre, and we moved to the village of Metjendorf in 1929. The next year, before I turned ten, he enrolled me at a secondary school for boys, the Gymnasium in Oldenburg, and took me there himself on the first day. To take the bus, operated by the German Post, hence called "*Post Auto*," would have cost almost one mark for the two of us, and after inflation, money was worth a lot again. We went on our bikes. The Gymnasium's curriculum was oriented toward humanistic education in the Classics, teaching obligatory Latin, Greek, and French, whereas the subjects of English, Spanish, or Hebrew were options later on. I became a sextaner, a student of the Sexta, the lowest level class. We were distinguished by the colours of our hat bands; in the spring, a differently coloured cap would indicate a pass into the next grade, the Quinta. Father took my academic education very seriously and started, simultaneously, to teach himself Latin with Langenscheidt's self-study course.

Unexpectedly, the principal of the neighbouring Ofen School, Herr Middendorf, became ill and had to be absent for several weeks. In addition to teaching, Herr Middendorf was the organist of the church located in Ofen. He knew father well and asked him to take over his organist chores for that period. There was, however, one unforeseen difficulty; to play the organ was not a matter of merely flicking a switch. Electrically driven bellows had not yet been introduced. Father's prosthesis had no intrinsic power either to play the organ foot keys or to pump the bellows. That was how I ended up performing this unfamiliar service; it became my task to keep the wedge bellows well and smoothly inflated while Father at the organ carried the choral tunes for the congregation. At age nine, unfortunately, I was not quite heavy enough for the task and to assist gravity, I had to pull down hard to obtain enough air pressure. During the Sunday service, I pulled too hard, jarring the bellows, and the organ, for a few measures, issued a vibrating, quivering sound, a strange contrast to Martin Luther's rock-solid "A Mighty Fortress Is Our God." Although nothing ever came of this incident, strangely enough, organ music has impressed me ever since.

The Sexta, my first class at the Gymnasium. Alphabetical seating placed me into the right front. The picture on the back wall is an old painting of the Greek Acropolis.

Wearing a Brunssen raincoat, in scuffed Bata shoes, briefcase at hand, ready to mount my bike for the five- mile ride to school.

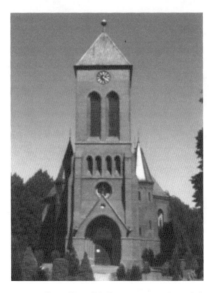

The church in Ofen, scene of my dismal failure as an underweight organ bellows pumper.

Gerd Asche

Years later, while studying medicine in Bonn, I attended many organ recitals, mostly at the Bonn-Poppelsdorf and Endenicher churches. I listened to Bach's Toccatas, the Passacaglia in C, Preludes and Fugues, although other, more modern organ music composers, Saint-Saens or Cesar Frank, are also my favourites. I learned of Arp Schnitger, a renowned 17th century local organ builder whose creations are found in hundreds of churches as far away as Portugal. The Schnitger organ in the Hamburg Jacobi Church, the largest in Germany, was restored recently and is of significance to me because my brother Kurt attended the official re-installation shortly before we lost him to pancreatic cancer.

Father playing Martin Luther's "Mighty Fortress of God" on the church organ contrasted with the reality of secular life at that time. The years following World War I in Germany marked the first attempt at a federal constitutional democracy. The Weimar Republic faced overwhelming challenges, stemming mainly from the harsh terms of the Versailles Peace Treaty. Train after train of high-quality anthracite coal and iron ore left for French and Belgian smelters. Huge portions of German land had been ceded to the neighbours Poland, France, Italy, Denmark, and Belgium. The Bayer pharmaceutical company lost the proprietary rights to its trade name and the intellectual and patent right to the synthesis of Aspirin. French troops were to occupy the Rhineland for fifteen years, and the right bank of the Rhine was to be kept demilitarized. Limits had been placed on the size of the military. The immense war reparations created serious financial problems for the people. The payments to France alone caused such a shortage of money that the government was forced to issue a *"Not Verordnung,"* an emergency decree, imposing a painful reduction of all civil servant and teacher salaries. Mother was indignant at having to make do with so much less, changing from dairy butter to margarine, switching off the electricity at night, and mending, rather than replacing, our torn clothes. The *"Not Verordnung" of the* twenty-three percent salary cut was what the opposing Nazi party had been waiting for; It would cost the governing Weimar Republic its life.

How dictates from above can impact everyone below. A photograph of Father attending a reunion with his teacher varsity colleagues shows the gentlemen wearing suits with a *Vorhemd*, a false shirt front. Known as a *chemiset* in French, this substitute had been introduced by the Huguenots who had fled Catholic France in the seventeenth century. Made of white plastic, with imitation pleats and buttons, the *chemiset* could be cleaned within minutes under cold water with soap and a stiff brush. Once it was dried off and reapplied, its bearer could proclaim the full dignity of wearing a brand-new fresh shirt. In the 1920s, the *Vorhemd* was indispensable for waiters in good restaurants, musicians in the orchestra pit of the opera, and teachers in country schools such as Adolf Asche, a principal who, despite the cut in his wages, tried to keep up his sartorial standing in the rural community.

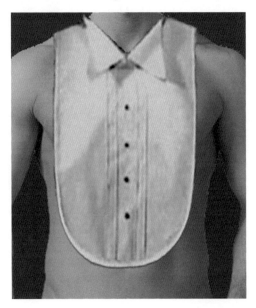

During the Depression, while a postage stamp cost a thousand marks, a *chemiset* was an inexpensive "false front" for impoverished gentlemen who had their income cut by twenty-three percent.

Gerd Asche

Father, the photographer, seated at the extreme left, had but a few seconds to reach his chair before the wound-up control would release his camera shutter and take the picture of the distinguished, chemiset-wearing assembly.

Father took the photograph of the distinguished-looking pedagogic dignitaries in the dining room of the Oldenburg Restaurant Ziegelhot, "The Brickyard," which catered to small group meetings. The twenty men must have enjoyed their modest *Mittag Essen* (noontime meal) of *Schweine Braten* (roast pork), boiled potatoes, red cabbage flavoured with apple and caraway, a custard for dessert, and perhaps a glass of Riesling Rhine wine. As veterans, survivors of the trenches, still remembering their field-grey uniforms, they had preserved a sense of solidarity, of brotherhood. In their dark suits, the teacher's professional attire, sign of erudition and modest prosperity, they were the intellectual leaders of their community. No one was too embarrassed sporting the *chemiset* instead of a starched linen shirt, but no one displayed any past war medals on their lapel. Civil servants all, they would have arrived on their bikes, some dependent on the use of an artificial arm or leg, taking hours from the far end of the Ammerland District, to this, their anniversary reunion, to discuss the recent salary cut and whether an appeal to the Minster of Churches and Schools might rescind the harsh measure.

For his photography, Father did not use flash powder; it was too unpredictable and might cost him the price of one expensive photographic glass plate. Instead, he took the picture by daylight in the dining room. A chair reserved in the front row, bottom left, would allow him time to reach his place with his artificial leg, before the ten-second wind-up released the shutter of the camera.

The practicality of the *chemiset*, the *Vorhemd*, solved the dilemma between the inability to afford fine shirts and the urge and obligation to be neat and respectable, although not always faultless in appearance. My father's *Vorhemd* was as much a part of his personal accoutrements as was his artificial leg; both were taken off for the night and reapplied in the morning. The fashion accessory was also symbolic; the fact that most of the distinguished gentlemen in the photograph were wearing the *Vorhemd* is evidence of both their shortage of means and their willingness to maintain their dignity by applying a false front. Nevertheless, the Ministry of Churches and Schools denied their appeal for a salary raise. Later, during the 1933 election, a good number of the teachers would vote for the Nazis who came up with better promises. At the next class reunion they would be wearing proper shirts and the Nazi Party pin attached to their lapel, and who could blame them for following the adage, "if you can't beat 'em, join them"?

The ruling Social Democrats had barely maintained the largest number of seats in a multi-party Reichstag through the 1920s. In addition, the unpopular economic measures of the Weimar government had fuelled the oppositions' standing. As conditions worsened after the stock market crash of 1929 and the Great Depression swept the globe, the Social Democrats became more and more the scapegoats, paying the price for shouldering the burden of a war instigated by the German royal family, by a Kaiser who had abdicated and fled the country for neutral Holland. The Social Democrats were blamed for having accepted German responsibility for the war and for putting their signature on the peace treaty. The German official who volunteered to sign, Matthias Erzberger, paid with his life for the thankless task. His murderers, although glorified by the Nazis, were brought to justice only after World War II.

Waiting in the wings was the overwhelming opposition group, the National Socialist Party, the Nazis, led by Austrian-born Adolf Hitler. In 1932, the Nazis became the party with the most elected seats. In January of 1933, Hitler was appointed Chancellor, and over the next few months, he succeeded through Machiavellian devices to eliminate much of his opposition and gain popularity by playing upon feelings of dissatisfaction and resentment. He was not averse to using terrorist tactics to further the cause. Brutality, purges, incarceration, and assassinations were part of the Party arsenal contributing to considerable political upheaval during Hitler's 1933 rise to power. The Nazi Party's solicitation for membership was a simple rhyme, convincing and Teutonic: *"Willst Du nicht mein Bruder sein, schlag ich Dir den Schädel ein."* (If you refuse to be my brother, I will smash in your skull.)

The new Nazi government decreed significant changes in the conduct of national assemblies and celebrations. In addition to the original "Germany" anthem with the melody from the Austrian composer Joseph Haydn, an additional harsh, political anthem, glorifying the swastika flag and mourning the party's dead heroes, became law. Both were to be sung in succession with the obligation that all participants had to raise their arm in the Hitler salute during the second anthem of "Die Fahne Hoch," (Raise the Swastika Banner). Mother, caught once in the midst of a demonstration, complained of the exertion to keep her arm raised throughout the duration; she had to support her right arm with the left hand. Backed by Nazi organizations such as *Sturm Abteilung* (SA) and the feared *Schutz Staffel* (SS), both para-military groups originally designated as Hitler's personal bodyguard, Der Führer openly promoted rearmament and campaigned for the suspension of reparations payments.

Father, burdened with his disabling war injury, was not in favour of all the martial propaganda, whether it came from the Nazis or from the right-wing veterans organization "Stahl *Helm*," the Steel Helmets. He resented the Nazis' flouting freedom of speech, violating human rights, and their demand to re-militarize the Rhineland, where, at France's request, German soldiers were *verboten*. The Nazis were calling for an increase in the number of German troops, which the Versailles Treaty had restricted to 100,000. Father had seen and felt on his own body the consequences of war and all its false glorifications. Accordingly, his propensity, although he never espoused the ideology of extreme socialism, was more toward the political left, in sympathy with the Social Democrats who were now the black sheep.

The Nazi Party managed to rout all opposition. After the *Macht Ergreifung* (the Power Grab), they claimed to have won the election by a suspicious margin of 98 percent. In the small village of Metjendorf where the number of voters may have been fifty or so, the polling station was supervised by a uniformed member of Hitler's *Sturm Abteilung*, wearing a swastika armband. If the results were correct as announced, it would be easy to figure out who had voted "No" or who had abstained. Following the election, Father was identified as a "Sozi," a socialist. Although he was far from favouring Marx's theory of a proletarian revolution, Father's "No" vote was directed against war and against those promoting it.

Father's parents had chosen his name Adolf in memory of the Scandinavian King Gustav Adolf II who was celebrated in northern Europe as the saviour of the Protestant religion at the end of the Thirty Years' War. King Gustav Adolf's Swedish troops had brought peace to war-torn Germany. Derived from *adelphos*, Greek for brother, the word Adolf is conspicuous in the ethical name of Philadelphia, the city of brotherly love. Three hundred years after Gustav Adolf II, the second "Adolf" arrived from abroad, from Austria, boasting of even greater achievements, promising liberation from the yoke of reparations, claiming to be the saviour of the Third Reich for a thousand years. Father, instead of showing the pride of bearing the name of a great man, resented the mountebank Adolf Hitler, the charlatan. Embarrassed, he felt that the good name had been degraded into a pejorative liability. Yet, he never made deprecating remarks about the only attribute he shared with Der Führer, the five letters of his first name.

That election in March, 1933, in which the Nazi Party achieved a majority, signalled war to Father. The entire Nazi movement meant war. By defaulting on reparations payments, the new government would have the money to prepare for armed conflicts and conquests. Father had voted "No" as a protest against war, but speaking his mind openly would have ended his career and could possibly have resulted in his immediate arrest. People disappeared silently, and no one really knew what happened to the victims. To talk freely became risky; everyone looked over the shoulder first to check for unwanted eavesdroppers. In the new rulers' eyes, those speaking out against war were speaking out against the Nazis; they were anti-Nazis, traitors, and enemies of the State. Although Father kept his political opinions to himself, his silence made him a marked man.

After the Easter holidays, a directive arrived from the Reichs Department of Enlightenment and Propaganda in Berlin, the previous Ministry of Churches and Schools, affecting all teachers of educational institutions—public and private schools, secondary, religious, and trade schools, gymnasia, universities, kindergarten and day care, whether teaching Latin, Chinese, music, ballet, engineering, skiing, or hairdressing. The new law, effective immediately, demanded that every classroom display a picture of Der Führer and that the Nazi salute precede every teaching lesson. Upon the teacher's entering, the students were to rise and stand at attention; the teacher, at the front of the room, was to assume a disciplined posture and, raising his right arm, to address the class with "Heil Hitler!" The students, arms raised, would respond in like fashion and the session could begin. Prayers were still allowed but the Almighty's place was second to the

Führer's, following the Hitler salute. On the day when the new regulation was introduced at the Gymnasium, it was obvious that some of our teachers disliked this puppet obligation. However, school teachers were civil servants and the ceremony was to become part of their duty.

I realized that what was imposed on my teachers at the Gymnasium in Oldenburg would also apply to my father, the teacher at the country school in Metjendorf. When I came home from school that afternoon, I wondered how father had fared under the Nazi ruling. He had not complied and was indignant at being directed to become a tool of the Nazis, propagating their politics. Before radio and telephone were common, a school teacher held a pivotal position in a small community. Thus, to the Party, teachers could be an asset, imbuing students with their propaganda; if a teacher were of a different political persuasion, however, he could "poison" the minds of Germany's youth and thus block the dissemination of Nazi ideology. Father would not, and never did, allow the name of the arrogant politician Adolf Hitler to cross his lips. Strangely, his omission of the Hitler salute did not seem to evoke the feared immediate action. Nobody came to arrest him; Father kept teaching as before without the prescribed protocol, and the authorities appeared to tolerate his intentional omission.

It was not known publicly that immediately following Hitler's election in 1933, the notorious SS General Heydrich, who was later eliminated by Czech patriots, and his successor General Kaltenbrunner, established the *Reichs Sicherheits Haupt Amt* (the RSHA, Reichs Security Head Office), of which six departments, Amts, looked after state security. Amt IV, under SS *Obergruppenführer* Heinrich Müller, opened a GeStaPo (*Geheime Staats Polizei*, secret state police) office in Oldenburg to deal with "subversive dissemination of state-hostile information."

Meanwhile, Father continued to teach without paying the demanded homage to the Führer. One day, a police car drove up. A Herr Becker and other officials from Amt IV began to visit him at our home. Father never spoke to us about the meetings; we did not know the purpose and assumed them to concern his salary and an increase in his disability pension. However, after Becker's first call, Father was forced to stop teaching, and had to see a Nazi-designated psychiatrist in Oldenburg who prescribed phenobarbital and chloral hydrate,which Father never took; the drugs, he felt, would poison his mind and his clear thinking. He became withdrawn, suspicious, and somewhat obsessive-compulsive, brushing his teeth and tongue frequently.

Our residence in Metjendorf, similar to the one in Godensholt, was part of the school building. The hallway received very little natural light from the front entrance corridor at a right angle to the long axis. Not wanting to burn expensive electricity, Father had devised a low voltage transformer to convert the German 220 volt current to 6 volts, feeding a small light bulb, just enough to be able to see at night. The little lamp also illuminated a painting that Father had copied of *Man in a Golden Helmet,* an impressive portrait, spuriously ascribed to Rembrandt. To make the imperfection of his work less noticeable, Father had hung it next to the inadequate light source where it was barely visible at night. In a whimsical way we accepted the helmeted old warrior as the symbolic guardian of our home, one of the *Lares,* the house deities, I had learned about at the Gymnasium in ancient Latin and Roman religion. Our "Lar," too, was there to observe, protect, and influence all that happened under its tiled roof. Although the guardsman's face was barely perceptible, the golden colour of his helmet, symbol of authority and order, retained a glow of its own in the penumbral passageway.

Father's copy of The Man in the Golden Helmet.

Early in the morning of November 10, 1933, Mother called me out of bed. "Father does not answer me; he is in there, in our *gute stube*," the room kept for special occasions; "he's locked himself in." She again knocked at the closed living room door and called: "Adolf, why don't you answer me?"

I sensed panic in Mother's voice. I got up, passed the little hall light, not noticing that the picture had been turned to face the wall. I pressed down the handle to the last door to the left, our *gute stube*. It was locked. I bent down, trying to look through the keyhole. It was clear; the key had been removed. All I could see was Father's nightshirt and his solitary leg protruding from it, like the clapper from a church bell, and I thought of the Ofen church where he had played the organ. As if by a hidden draft, his body was rotating gently. It was my father! In a panic I shot away from the door. "Er hängt! Er hängt!"

There was no telephone; Mother took her bike to call Herr Heeren, a friend and owner of the nearby mill and feed store, who came immediately and summoned some helpers. Opa Schütte came from Tweelbäke.

He gave us comfort: "*Der Herr hat's gegeben, der Herr hat's genommen, sein Name sei gelobt.*" (The Lord giveth and the Lord hath taken away; blessed be the name of the Lord.) There was nothing else he could do or say but exhort us to praise the Lord. "Your father did not want a silent witness on his way to Golgotha," he said, when he turned back the picture of the man with the golden helmet. Then he had to leave to milk the cows.

Mother had become a widow, and my brothers and I were fatherless now. No longer would I have my mentor in Latin, no longer was he there if I needed advice and guidance, and no longer did I have to put up with his restrictive discipline.

A letter arrived from the RSHA, the Nazi justice department. In pretended generosity, the Attorney General's office had gracefully waived an inquest and post-mortem examination. They had successfully concluded this unmanageable case and did not need to determine the cause of death. Another package arrived, containing a distasteful *memento mortis* with a clipping of Father's death notice glued to the bottom of a translucent glass ashtray and a request for a three mark donation. No one came to speak to us. The public budget of the Weimar Republic did not include social services or counseling. People had always coped without such assistance; we, therefore, did not miss it.

The funeral was at the *Neue Friedhof*, the new cemetery. I remember some men shaking my hand. Their words sounded very sincere, I don't remember their names; they may have been the members of "Sangest Lust," the old Godensholt men's choir Father had organized and had been conducting. On the next day when Mother went to the funeral home to pay the bill, she expressed her surprise that she had heard a brass band tuning up to Chopin's Funeral March at the grave-side, an extra expense she had not expected. In a hypocriti-cal tone, the clerk assured her evasively not to be concerned; the band had been requested and paid for by Amt IV of the government "to honour one of its former civil servants and a decorated war veteran."

As for me, I never got over what Father had done. I never forgave him and, during the remaining years I lived in Germany, never visited his grave. However, in hindsight, pondering his action from something other than a child's point of view, some facts have gained a new significance. On one occasion, he had taken me aside and admonished me to take care of Mother and my brothers. At the time such a rebuke seemed unimportant and odd; the prognostic significance of this gesture did not sink in. I now know that it was a message from a man who knew he would have to leave us.

Father was not afraid of dying; he had faced death before when his leg was torn off in northern France, and although he made the preparations for his departure diligently, he was probably unaware of the more humane "long drop" used in punitive hanging which dislocates the neck vertebrae, causing almost instant cessation of life. Instead, he suffered a slow death by strangulation and choking. His planning would have involved deciding upon a point of suspension high enough to keep his body off the floor. Achieving his departure must have been difficult with only one leg, without using a noisy stepladder. It would have to be at night when everyone was asleep. He would have to be very quiet. He could not wear his leg prosthesis because he required his wife's help to strap it on. He would have to get out of bed silently and hop bare-foot on one leg along the cold concrete hallway floor, past the little light and the man in the golden helmet, to reach the living room. He would have to keep his balance while placing a chair on top of the dining table, then, dependent on only one leg, he would have to climb the table. Holding on to the backrest, he would have to get up to stand on his one leg on the chair, reach for the lamp hook on the ceiling to insert the end of the rope, loop the noose around his neck, allowing sufficient length for him to dangle, and then step off the chair.

At the time, we saw Father's act as totally irrational. We did not connect it to his contrary political views. Speaking out in favour of the Nazis could perhaps have saved his life, but he would never be willing to make that spineless concession. We thought he may have taken this step out of selfishness, because of the suffering caused by his physical handicap. We may have thought, albeit very remotely, that his death could have been Gestapo-induced. However, we never connected the loss of his position and the visits from party officials with a cleverly bullied political suicide.

These were very upsetting days. I don't know how much the incident affected my younger brothers; I suppose the facts were kept from them for some time. Eighty years ago, we resented more than deplored Father's departure. He left no farewell note, no letter of comfort or apology, no life insurance policy, no savings account. He just left, dropping the responsibility for raising three immature boys into our mother's lap. For twenty years, I never discussed his death, but I thought about it many times. Later, after my medical training, I sought a pathological explanation. I considered depression as a cause of Father's choosing to end his life. However, there was no previous occurrence of such a condition in his family, nor have symptoms of emotional disorder or despondency emerged in any of us, his progeny. Nor was he suffering from schizophrenia or depressive bipolar disorder. More recently, I have considered the now fashionable diagnosis of long-lasting post-traumatic stress disorder. However, Father showed no signs of this condition. Was it perhaps a silent signal of reprimand, directed at us? Without thinking of Becker's political torments Father may have had to endure, I was angry at him, a man who obviously was intelligent enough to realize the burden his act was shifting on to Mother. I regret now that

I never gave much thought to how his action had affected her. I don't think she expected any sympathy. She never showed her emotions to us, but allowed and tolerated and never criticized my resentment at Father's decision. We never asked her how she felt. She was a remarkable woman from a stolid Methodist family who could take a lot of stress. Only now am I beginning to understand how my Father could have done what he did, conferring on us, his sons, the status of the boys and girls in the Waisen Haus where he grew up, making us fatherless orphans also.

Thirty-five years later, as a Canadian, when I revisited Oldenburg and my brothers, I was somewhat mellowed and reconciled and went to the cemetery. I looked for Father's tombstone in vain. My brother Kurt explained that since I had never expressed any interest, they had allowed the title to the plot to lapse; both grave and headstone were no longer. It hurt me to learn that the same had been done with Mother's grave but then, as an immigrant in far-away Canada where I was under considerable professional pressure, I never assumed any responsibility and had left all obligations to my two brothers.

Chapter 3

It was after the Easter break, back in 1930, three years before the Nazis took over, when Father had enrolled me at the age of nine at the Oldenburg Gymnasium. In compliance with the original meaning of "gymnasium," the curriculum contained a degree of physical education but the preponderance of instruction was classical languages. The school was located in the "*Alte Palais*," the old palace, the previous residence of the Oldenburg Grand Duke's family on the "*Damm*," referring to ancient town fortifications. Some time after Father's death, under the new government, the conspicuous building housing the Gymnasium was forced to cede to the spirit of the "New Times"; it was appropriated for the headquarters of the Nazi Party's regional administration. The original Gymnasium was transferred to and combined with the "*Real Gymnasium*," a neoclassic institution, now amusingly called the *Alte Gymnasium,* a school where I spent my student years as a teenager and received a good humanistic education.

Here at the Gymnasium, I was exposed to the teaching by Studienrat Lübken who was a born teacher and pedagogue and who introduced us to *Ludus Latinus*, my first Latin textbook. In the class photograph, the absence of a Hitler picture on the wall confirms that it was taken before the Nazi era; my place, following the alphabetical rule, was in the first row, far to the right. Another teacher whom I enjoyed was Herr Sartorius. He bore the Latinized name of Schneider, meaning tailor, and was good at teaching drawing and art history. His fondness for the botanical flower paintings of the Dutch Masters, which he connected with his course in the biology of the Hunte River downs, awakened in me an interest in the birds and plants of the local wetlands and the beauty and value of antique flower paintings.

In addition to my lack of ambition to excel, my weakness was in mathematics. The teacher obviously had little interest in how or to whom he taught algebra or trigonometry. One of the teachers, Herr Braun, remains in my memory because he was tall and liked to walk along the aisle between us seated students. Because of his height, the most notable part of his features was what is called the inguinal area. His trousers showed pronounced urine stains. He probably did not take the time to wait for the urine stream to cease and let the final portion run into his trousers and his underwear, if there was any. However, in retrospect, and now with medical knowledge, I realize we may have been condemning him unjustly. He may have been afflicted with a congenital abnormality such as an inoperative urinary hypospadia that impairs the control of urinary excretion, but our ignorance led us to the harmless ridicule of he unfortunate man. More important was our development of a second sense for distinguishing a convinced Nazi or a dangerous political fanatic; he would use the words "Der Führer" or "our Führer in contrast to the generic word :government," or simply "Hitler." These people could be dangerous, and caution was advised in our conversations. Mr. Ali Brockmann, the teacher in charge of our physical education, was one member of the staff whom we did not trust. We did not know if his frequent use of the word *Der Führer* was pretended political enthusiasm to obtain and retain his non-academic position, or if he was a convinced Nazi, even a political spy, who would denounce us and his fellow teachers. We were always careful in our conversations with him.

Another teacher of controversial features was Doktor Naumann who taught French and English as well as literature. I remember his discussing the writer Henrick Ibsen's *Hedda Gabler,* the story of a woman unhappy and frustrated with her middle class existence who derives satisfaction from manipulating those around her. Herr Naumann demonstrated Ibsen's dramatization of the struggle between the inward desires of his characters and the restriction of their social environments. He showed to us students the theme of late 19th century feminism; its chastising the overbearing bourgeois society fit well into the Nazi philosophy. Herr Naumann also pointed out Ibsen's use of symbolism, including the hair as a sign of potency and Hedda's envy of Thea's abundant endowment. Although none of us really knew what the term meant, Dr. Naumann was quite able to convey to us uninitiated teenagers that Hedda was a "fallen woman" and how she came to be one. Like the protagonist in a recent book by Redelf, Herr Naumann, *Nauke* to us, had nicotine-stained fingers, poor oral hygiene, and a frequent repulsive retro-nasal grunting, suggesting a post-nasal obstruction which I later re-discovered in the comic cartoon of *Beavis and Butthead.* Nauke's self-neglecting appearance, wearing dandruff-flecked dark blue suits with stained lapels, was enhanced by a waddling gait, suggestive of a congenital hip dislocation. After the war my brother Kurt sent me Redelf's book "*Staatsfeinde*" (*Enemies of the State*), pointing out certain similarities to Naumann. Although his name is not mentioned, it appears that Naumann could be the protagonist of the publication. (*Staatsfeinde: ein Roman Zwischen 1933 und 1945/* Hans Fr. Redelfs – Oldenburg: Holzberg 1989. Heinz Holzberg Verlag KB, Oldenburg.) In fairness to Herr Naumann, he did teach me an excellent French pronunciation which put me in good stead when I started interpreting during the war in France. His linguistic influence on me extends into his teaching of English pronunciation that sets me apart from the guttural accent displayed by many German immigrants.

Our teacher in chemistry and physics, a senile but kind professor, "Putz" Willers, still commenced his morning lessons with "*Anfang, Mitte, und Ende, Herr Gott, in Deine Hande,*" Beginning, middle and end, Lord, are in your hands. Although under the new directive the Hitler salute had to precede prayers, it seemed that Professor Willers was trying to mitigate the effect of the crude Nazi indoctrination by his spiritual admonitions. We were, of course, rascals and made his life difficult. He sometimes took me aside, appealing to my conscience and asking me to think of my poor mother. He meant well but his admonitions did not sink in. His lectures in electronics and chemistry, however, were interesting, and I tried to repeat some of the more impressive chemical reactions at home on Bremer Chaussee 37.

Herr Eggerking, a gentleman, a scholar, and an outstanding teacher, taught the classic Greek of the *Odyssey,* the poem in which Homer recounts the wanderings and return of Odysseus or Ulysses from Troy to his home in Ithaca. Herr Eggerking was a war veteran and bachelor, and there was rumour that as a result of a war injury he had lost one or both testicles. He did not strike me as an emasculated eunuch; he could take care of an unruly class very effectively. Dr. Eggerking was well liked; I owe him a substantial debt for his teaching classical Greek and Latin. He certainly was not a pro-Nazi. However, both the teacher and we students had to be careful of some of our own classmates, in particular Helmuth Warmboldt and Hans Alberts, who were Hitler Youth leaders and fanatics. I don't think that any of these misguided boys survived their useless enthusiasm and sacrifice during the war. One of them, seduced by the glorified prospect of a U-boat officer's career, dropped out prematurely. He was lost at sea and, as his classmates, we had to hold a brief memorial service.

Most of the German songs, the *Lieder,* I learned through Herr Storkebaum, our music teacher, who had organized a small school orchestra which I heard play one of the Brandenburg concertos in the auditorium. I was very impressed and whenever I hear the "Brandenburgs" I always subconsciously remember the school orchestra playing the music of J.S. Bach. Storkebaum had also arranged for some of us to sing in the choir during the Easter *St. Matthew's*

Passion performance in the local Garrison Church and later in the big Lamberti Kirche. I received a remuneration of ten marks for the season for my participation as a soprano in the choir. Since this introduction, I have not forgotten this monumental work and consider Bach's music sacred, symbolic of my ethnic heritage.

I had a brief stint in the Staats Theatre as a stage hand and on one occasion took part in "acting" during the performance of Modest Mussorgsky's opera *Boris Godunov.* The script calls for a child to be carried in on a shield. The real stage hand, a smaller boy, was sick, and I offered to be the substitute. At fourteen, I was certainly not small, being of good weight, but I was badly needed and available on that night. I remember that the shield bearers inadvertently dropped me on stage because I was much heavier than they expected. I slid off the shield gently, holding on to the edge, as if it were part of the drama. In the half-dark of the stage, only a few in the audience noticed the deviation from the classical script. That night, I made ten marks extra.

My interest in chemistry led me to convert a small attic room on Bremer Chaussee into a laboratory. Here I concocted some minor test tube reactions with potassium permanganate. The explosions of hydrogen gas, which were more spectacular than I had seen Professor Willers demonstrate, caused no damage to the window or the building. Less spectacular was my main interest, electronics, which was then just developing. Some parts, transformers and tubes, were left from Father's hobby legacy, but I was short of the funds to build a real radio. My efforts always yielded near-misses but worked so-so; all I could receive were German broadcasts.

I was always interested in amateur radio as a source of news from abroad. When a new government order required secondary school pupils to be members of the Hitler *Jugend,* the Hitler Youth, to avoid expulsion from school, I went to see an older student, Gunther F., who was in charge of the local communications group. He was not politically oriented and held a coveted ham radio licence; his father, also a school-teacher, was a member of the *Stahl Helm* (Steel Helmet) veteran's organization until it was disallowed by the Nazis. The function of the Hitler Jugend signals unit was to organize and provide sound systems for larger youth group meetings but otherwise nobody made political demands. I was accepted, and we spent that summer on the North Sea island of Wangerooge operating the sound systems for a large Hitler *Jugend* camp while staying in tents on the beach. Nobody ordered us to attend their rallies, to participate in indoctrinations, or to join in the singing of party songs about Nazi heroes, and we enjoyed our freedom.

Although I could steer clear of politics, the camp on Wangerooge was the location of my first encounter with a homosexual who used his authority as the leader of our group to gain access. He approached me in our tent at night; I woke up when he took my penis and was manipulating it. It was a shaming and unpleasant new experience but I have come to no physical or emotional trauma as so many nowadays claim they have. I was probably fourteen or fifteen at the time. I returned to school after the summer holidays.

Apart from Mr. Brockmann, the physical education instructor who seemed a Nazi fanatic, the rest of the teachers at the Gymnasium were intellectuals and at least not active party members. But the Nazi Party did manage to insert itself into our school life beyond the observance of the classroom "Heil Hitler" ritual and compulsory membership in the Hitler Youth. Subtle revisions to history were made to help dovetail it with the Nazi ideology. Arminius (Hermann), the great German leader who had stopped the Romans at the Weser River, whose monument Father and I had visited some ten years previously, was reduced to a footnote in the new history textbooks. While Father had proclaimed him a national hero who had saved the Germanic countries from the domination by Latin culture, Goebbels' Nazi propaganda machine made disappointingly little of Arminius. The statue itself, facing west as it does, was said to have been erected to celebrate Germany's victory over France in the Franco-Prussian War of 1870/71. As Italy was now an ally, Hitler chose to tread carefully. Mussolini was touchy, especially in matters about the controversial Italian conquest of Ethiopia and about his nation's past, particularly Roman wars and battles lost. Instead of praising German superiority in Arminius' defensive success against the Legions, the new history books deplored the "loss of opportunities for cultural enrichment and trade." Little did I suspect, reading about them in my high school text-books, how my own destiny within a few short years would take me into the territories of both the former enemy, France, and the new ally, Italy, wearing a German army uniform.

My teenage years at the Gymnasium were relatively uneventful. My report card assessed me as "gifted, but easily distracted by attempting to accomplish too many tasks." My marks went down. I do not know if Father's violent death and our losing the head of our family contributed to my poor scholastic performance. I can conveniently blame it. I had to repeat courses on two occasions. Ordinarily I might have been expelled, but Father's having been a teacher colleague and a distinguished veteran with a major war injury, the rumoured mode of his departing, and Mother's status as a teacher's widow with three boys were all taken into consideration and spared me paying the high price of losing my privilege to attend the Gymnasium. Through the grapevine, some of the "old school" of the teaching staff may have been aware of the brutal psychological pressure tactics used by the Gestapo to enforce Nazi doctrine on non-compliant teachers, resulting in other suicides. Certainly, they understood, more than I did myself, the cause of my academic decline. Their votes saved me from expulsion. Although a failing student's compliment for his teacher is meaningless and unlikely to be appreciated, I hold the memories of those teachers favouring my academic progress in high esteem.

Looking back now, I realize how little I was aware of Father's past at that time. Indeed, it was only recently that I read in an old newspaper that he had been the recipient of the prestigious Iron Cross decoration. He had never mentioned the award to us; neither had he shown us the medal nor told the story of his alleged bravery. He had his nose full of the snot of war. Perhaps that was also part of the reason for his deliberate departure. Perhaps he could not face the possibility that his own three sons would not escape a similar fate in the coming years. I do regret that I reviled my Father's bizarre action for so many years. I now appreciate how my ability to investigate the details of his story and to write about them is a legacy inherited from the stalwart country schoolteacher.

Chapter 4

Once Father's funeral was behind us, nothing kept us in Metjendorf. Mother found a modest two-bedroom upstairs apartment on the outskirts of Oldenburg with closer access to her Methodist friends and a shorter distance to our schools. The novelty and diversions of urban life made up for our loss of country freedom and Mother's straightened circumstances. She could no longer afford to buy our groceries in quantity and often had to send us to the butcher for ground meat or sausage for one meal at a time, or for half a pound or a pound of flour, sugar, or other items not worth the grocer's cost of a paper bag. We would come home with the sugar in a substitute tapered container, rolled out of a sheet of newspaper.

Our living space was restricted. The odoriferous non-flush toilet was accessed from the stairwell and Mother admonished us constantly to replace the wooden lid and keep the door closed. As teenage girls endure the menarche, the beginning of menstrual periods, so had I, as a boy, to put up with "wet dreams," nocturnal emissions, in a bedroom shared with my brother. I paid little attention to the experience, except for Mother's esoteric scoldings of being too lazy to get up and her fretting about "knowing better than to wet the bed at my age."

On Saturday evenings, the common laundry kitchen downstairs became our bath room for the once-a-week ablution. The water remained in the zinc tub and was kept warm by successive additions from the laundry kettle until all had bathed. Kurt, the youngest, presumed the least polluted, was the first one, and Mother the last. Assuming that the process of washing is one of dilution, we still emerged cleaner. An extra cleansing for my body was included in our school curriculum as a weekly swimming lesson at the city's well-chlorinated indoor pool. It was a good excuse to skip the awkward tub bath on Saturdays. Despite her reduced widow's income, Mother managed to keep up the payments for secondary education for all three of us. However, school holidays made the apartment too crowded, and I spent a good deal of my free time with my grandparents.

In Varel, after Opa Asche's passing, Oma and Tante Ida had changed from their very comfortable residence in the Waisen Haus to an attic apartment with a spare bedroom on Oster Strasse. To visit them from Oldenburg took me about two hours on my bike. The first landmark to come into sight was the water tower which had played such a prominent role on the day of my birth. At a height of fifty metres, it offered a view as far as the North Sea coast.

From Oma's place, I would also visit my aunt and uncle, the Neefs, whose son, my cousin Hans, worked as an electrical engineer in Wilhelmshaven, Germany's naval base with access to the North Sea and the Atlantic. In the morning, Hans would pack his lunch kit and walk to the nearby station, have his breakfast on the train, and be at the Wilhelmshaven shipyards on time to pursue his research on improving the efficiency of batteries used in U-boats. The provisions of the Versailles Peace Treaty at the end of World War I had included, along with major territorial losses to France, Poland, Italy, Denmark, and Belgium, the prohibition against building submarines. Hans knew he was circumventing the treaty; it was an open secret that the Germans were flouting many restrictions of what we called the *Dictate* of Versailles, but government wages were good. I got along well with my cousin Hans, discussing chemistry and electronics, until he died from acute leukemia, probably contracted from inhalation of toxic electrolyte fumes at the shipyard's laboratory.

From Oma's place I would also ride my bike to the small seaport of Vareler Hafen to go swimming, taste the saltwater, feel it burn my eyes, and experience the pungent smell of curing shrimp emanating from the Garnelen Darre. Occasionally I would still visit my birthplace, the Waisen Haus.

Tante Ida suffered from an eye disease called glaucoma, a condition that was progressive. Despite her very thick, heavy glasses she was barely able to read the newspaper headlines. Trained as a stenographer and typist, she had to give up her work with the Opel automobile agency in Oldenburg which had a reputation comparable to General Motors in the United States. At one time, she had been engaged to Hermann Asche, a visiting American cousin, and move with him to the States, but her impaired vision thwarted the plans, and she remained single almost all her life. To a near-blind person with limited options, a radio would be of great advantage. However, the cost of such a novelty was prohibitive until Father built a receiver for Tante Ida and Oma Asche. His creation was a huge, self-contained sturdy box made of a new kind of wood consisting of sheets glued together, known as plywood. Stained dark and with a coat of varnish, it fit in well with the living room furniture. The built-in monster of a horn-type loudspeaker and the heavy transformers feeding electricity to the glass tubes explained the enormous size and weight of the set. I was awed by the accomplishment; it was Father's first dabbling in radio. I admired his skill, and his penchant for radios seems to have transferred to me. I became very interested in electronics and later built sophisticated amateur equipment and served as a communications technician during the war. Years later, after I had become a Canadian citizen, I attained a Canadian Amateur Radio licence with the unique call sign VE7AOK. I made many Morse-code and single-side-band voice contacts on short wave and visited other amateurs in Europe, Hawaii, the United states, Asia, and Australia, but that was twenty years later.

At Varel, my guest bedroom at Oma Asche's was located above the Behrens Tanzschule, and its loud piano music instructions kept me awake into the night. But sharp at 8:00

a.m., Oma would flick on Father's radio and wake me up with the *Nord West Deutsche* Radio's *(NWDR)Hafen Konzert* from Hamburg. From my bed, while listening to popular overtures by Franz Lehar, Carl Maria von Weber, the musical introduction to *Poet and Peasant* by Franz von Suppe, to Rossini's *Thieving Magple*, or *Die Fledermaus* (The Bat) by Johann Strauss, I could look across the Oster Strasse directly at an attractive red brick house owned and occupied by Herr Balzer and his family, a teacher of Latin and Greek. It seemed unusual that he was out of work at a time when there was a shortage of academic manpower. Rumour had it that his unemployment was due to "Jewish blood," a reason inexplicable to me. He looked and acted like everybody else and I asked myself how he could have acquired this undesirable attribute and what the reason was for his unspoken disbarment from teaching. When my school report showed a decline in Greek, Oma arranged coaching lessons for me. I spent some time in the red brick house under Herr Balzer's tutorship, paid for by Oma Asche. She never told me whether the money was to support the Balzers financially, to spite the cruel Nazi anti-Jewish policies, or to improve my standing in classical Greek. The Balzer's daughter Katharina, a dark-haired pleasant little girl of five, enjoyed interrupting our lessons. I never heard from the Balzers again and fear that Oma Asche's tuition fees neither kept the Balzer family out of the cremation chambers of Buchenwald concentration camp nor improved my shortcomings in Plato's writings or in Socrates' Apologia.

A few houses down Oster Strasse, a Mr. Charles Perrin kept a book store and rental library. He was said to be well-off, his house having been paid for mysteriously with Australian dollars. He was a dealer in antique postage stamps and coins; upon entering the Frenchman's house, customers could detect the penetrating odour of cats or rather of cats' urine. Renting books there occasionally, I did not foresee the role this ruffled eccentric would one day play in the Asche family.

During the last years of World War II, Charles Perrin and Tante Ida became mutually attracted. It may have been less romance and more a matter of convenience. He was a bachelor, alone with those cats for company, and Tante Ida, getting older and more visually impaired, needed companionship beyond that of her aging mother. While I was a soldier in Italy, in charge of the Siena TF post in Italy, Mother wrote that the two had become a couple and that Tante Ida had moved in with Charles. When they then took Oma Asche into their household, the first items to go were those cats. Next, the two women converted Charles to better grooming and personal hygiene and improved his housekeeping. However, there was one important convention, usually observed on such occasions, in which Tante Ida failed; she never persuaded Charles to make out a proper will. When the unexpected happened and Charles suddenly died, his not inconsiderable wealth ended up, to the chagrin of his newly acquired relatives, in the coffers of the government of the State of Lower Saxony. Looking back, I wonder why Tante Ida would not have been entitled to a widow's share of the estate. Had she perhaps lived with Charles in sin? The precious rascal had left no life insurance either, a fact I learned, along with news of Charles Perrin's interment and of the inheritance past praying for, long after the events.

During the last years of his life, Father had been an avid reader and a subscriber to a monthly book selection. Some books he acquired became my literature also: Sven Hedin's *From the Apennine to the Andes*, Edward Bulwer-Lytton's *The Last Days of Pompeii,* Scott's *Ivanhoe*, histories of Napoleon's retreat *From Moscow to the Beresina River*, the Scandinavian authors Selma Lagerloef and Bjornstern Bjornson, and the Baltic writer Hermann Sudermann, whose *Lithuanian Stories* would come again to my hands under dramatic circumstances. As soon as I could read, I had found under the Christmas tree my first literary adventures, Mark Twain's *Prinz und Bettelknabe* (The Prince and the Pauper), the story of Tom Sawyer, and the delightful trilogy of Sonnleitner's *Die Höhlenkinder (*the Cave Children). As my reading skills picked up and I advanced to Twain's adult-oriented *Selected Sketches*, I was horrified by the story of cannibalism that, in true cold Twain irony, castigated the quality of meals served on railway dining cars. The story goes as follows: On a train heading from St. Louis, the unnamed narrator meets a stranger who tells him a story about being stranded because of a blizzard with no way for the passengers to get help. The fascinating part of the story is that instead of starving from hunger, the men on the train decided to elect democratically which fellow sufferer would be eaten to provide food for the others. Their first choice, a Mr. Harris, they found tough and stringy. In all, they were stranded on the train for more than a week and the total of deaths due to cannibalism was around a dozen. I soon realized that Mark Twain wrote satirical fiction. Father, despite the shortness of money, had also kept up a subscription to *Westermann's Monats Hefte,* an expensive sophisticated periodical. He had enjoyed the odd good cigar while reading; he also used to copy landscape paintings by locally renowned artists and old masters such as the *Man In a Golden Helmet* which had hung in our hallway. The visits to my paternal grandmother Oma Asche in Varel kept me immersed in my father's world with its aura of sophisticated intellectual enrichment, which was enhanced by access to Charles Perrin's books, the musical radio entertainment, the continued exposure to classic languages through Herr Balzer, and even to the distinctive rhythm of the Tanz Schule's nocturnal Polkas, Foxtrots and Waltzes.

In contrast to Varel, visiting my maternal grandparents Schütte in Tweelbäke offered a more bucolic setting, coupled with greater spiritual values. Mother's parents were devout Methodists with a hand-stitched Old Testament sampler over their bed: "As for me and my house, we shall serve the Lord" (Joshua 24:15), A modest, pedal-powered harmonium stood in the large living and dining room, and at dinner time, while the food was carried in from the kitchen, Onkel Eduard played a hymn or two to heighten the family's pre-prandial anticipation. A simple prayer preceded the meal. The tea was strong; it had to be, to suppress the taste and odour of peat in the ground water obtained from the outdoors hand pump. Initially, when the Schüttes had bought the parcel of land, it was a peat bog; over the years they had drained and cleared it by hand, using the dried sods as fuel. The uncovered sandy soil grew rye, buckwheat, potatoes, and the ubiquitous kale, brassica oleracea, all their main sustenance.

Oma Schütte baked loaves of dark rye bread in a free-standing outdoor baking oven. Every farm usually had one of the small well-insulated caves built of bricks that required a hot fire of black peat. Once heated up, the fire was removed and the unbaked loaves inserted with a long-handled wooden spatula. The oven door was shut quickly to allow the remaining heat to bake the coarse sour dough rye meal. Sealing the hardwood oven door with clay was insufficient, resulting in heat loss when the clay dried and fell off. Better, but extravagant, was the use of bread dough; however, fresh cow dung provided the best heat retention and temperature consistency. This adhesive of digested grass stayed on if applied properly by hand and would allow the dough to bake into a fresh loaf of fragrant rye bread.   Peeled   potatoes were served boiled, mashed, or pan-fried in chopped bacon. Potato salad was reserved for festive occasions that justified the preparation of mayonnaise with eggs and rape seed oil. Unpeeled, boiled potatoes came with a meal of pickled salt herrings, a rare treat for people living away from the coast. The cows supplied milk and precious manure for the fields. Butter was spread sparingly, almost scraped, over the coarse slices of schwarz brot.

Slaughtering a pig was a festive occasion; long before thinking of my future plans to become a doctor and of human blood clots and strokes, I received a demonstration of how quickly fresh pig's blood will clot and become useless for the delicious crisp fried blood cakes, unless well stirred and agitated. My task was to keep the flies off the carcass strung up and spread open on a ladder to cool and be ready for the meat inspector to check for trichinosis.

For special occasions, the tea water was taken from a large rain barrel with the mosquito larvae wiggling just under the surface skimmed off. After proper boiling, there was nothing wrong with the tea without peat flavour, which was served with cream and sweetened with lumps of brown sugar crystals on cotton threads called Kandies. In general, the simpler the food, the more critical were the palates.

Opa Schütte spent a lot of time on me, his first grandson. He allowed me some trials at ploughing with his team of horses, Fanny and Flocky; however, the furrows I created were too crooked to qualify for his approval. During the July holidays, we, the grandchildren, were to help with the haying, using large, heavy, wooden rakes. Allthough we city boys were of little use, we worked up an appetite all the same and looked forward to the four o'clock break, called "Vesper," when Cousin Eleonore would arrive on her bike with sweet tea and black rye bread sandwiches, buttered and covered with smoked ham, slices of large sausages, or delicious smoked bacon. That would do us until six, the time for the evening meal, a plateful of bacon-fried potatoes. The milk, without cooling refrigeration or ice, was kept in the cellar; however, sour milk, allowed to curdle and covered with black bread crumbs and sugar, was a wonderful dessert on hot days. In the fall and winter, a pot of chopped kale, cooked with smoked sausage called *pinkel* or with smoked bacon, and served with boiled potatoes, was a feast. Beggars and visitors dropping in at mealtime were to join the family table. Sitting next to one such transient, I could smell his strong, slightly sour odour. For protection against robbers, Opa Schütte had a shotgun standing behind his bed; however, it never went into action. The Schüttes were cheerful, warm people, with a lot of harmonium music and hymn singing without hypocrisy; my mother must have had a happy, albeit austere childhood.

Oma Schütte, mother and mistress of the house, bore four children, Ernst and Eduard, Marie and Amalie, my mother. Oma was less outgoing; Opa was the driving force who told me that one of his ancestors, a compulsive gambler, had squandered the family farm. The great-grandchildren, of whom Opa was one, had to buy wild land and cultivate it by hand; building up again what their ancestor had played away. Playing cards had become the Devil's prayer book and were not allowed in the otherwise liberal house. For a small peat farmer, Opa Schütte was unusually erudite; he spoke a modicum of Latin and liked to quote Napoleon during his exile on St. Helena, off the coast of Africa, perhaps alluding to the first hard years he spent cultivating the land: "*Justitiam amavi et injustitiam odi; itaque in exilio moriar.*" (I have respected justice and hated injustice; in the end, I shall die in exile.)

The city of Oldenburg was six kilometres away. A large open square in the centre, called the *Pferde Markt*, the Horse Market, although large scale horse trading was long gone, was the location of the October entertainment. Called the *Kramer Markt*, with a roller coaster, merry-go-rounds, and the usual choice of amusements, the carousel's calliope music attracted me, and I spent hours listening to the wistful melodies from operas and folk songs. One October afternoon after Father's death (I was without funds, although I did not miss them), I was hanging around the *Kramer Markt* after school, enjoying the music with its worldly tunes of love and passion. Unexpectedly, who taps me on the shoulder but my Methodist Opa Schütte? And what does this God-fearing, righteous man do? He pulls from his vest pocket a shiny *Taler*, a silver three-mark piece, and hands it to me, just like that! It was a confidential and generous transaction of so much money, to be spent frivolously on worldly pleasures, obviously without the knowledge of Oma. The story of the spendthrift Schütte ancestor and a possible relapse of the prodigal son episode entered my mind. My always frugal Opa, who lived in a very small house, with the marital sleeping chamber too narrow to have their beds side-by-side, must have felt sorry for me, coming as he had, on his bicycle all the way from Tweelbäke to look for me, his first grandson, fatherless, penniless, and craving some fun. I wondered if he expended that kind of generosity on his other six grandchildren; to ask them could have invited a revolt among family members. I had no trouble wasting all the good money and still coming home hungry. The transaction bonded Opa and me and has remained our secret for life.

Some years after my immigration to British Columbia, I visited another member of the Schütte family who had moved to nearby Oregon. She was Opa's niece and, fittingly for the Schütte family tradition, the daughter of a Methodist pastor. An immigrant from Neuruppin, Germany, Henny Schütte, a photographer, was living in Hood River, Oregon, It was through Henny that we learned more about my origin--that before me, Mother had a miscarriage, a boy. We also learned that Tante Marie, Mother's older sister, had lived in Mother's shadow. She had been desperate to find a husband and was a rival for my father's affection. Despite his severe one-legged handicap, Father must have been an attractive proposition. Marie finally married an electrical engineer with two little girls from a previous marriage.

After World War II and a number of years in Canada, I returned to visit Germany and called on Tante Marie in an old folks' home near Oldenburg. She had not laid eyes on me for about two decades, but her memory had remained unimpaired. As I walked into the room filled with many beds and visitors, she recognized me immediately; before I had located her, she called me by my name.

Unlike most of my classmates at the Gymnasium, shortage of money made watching a movie at the local theatre, the "Kino," a rare treat for me. About a year before the Nazis came to power, a science fiction drama named "No Reply from FP1" was showing, and I begged Mother to allow me to go. Made before the colour-film era, it was about a floating city with an airport and other facilities similar to modern floating oil platforms, located in mid-Atlantic where transoceanic planes could land for refueling and repairs. English and French-language versions were also produced and highly advertised. I bought a cardboard cut-out and built my own FP1 model. The screenwriter, Kurt Siodmak, a German Jew, had escaped to Hollywood. After 1933, the Nazi government publicly burned Siodmak's books and took his movies out of circulation without reason other than that the author was born a Jew. It speaks for the film's quality and the impression it must have made on me that I remember it after seventy-five years.

The influence and power of Nazi propaganda also reached us in the Gymnasium. One day in June of 1936, all Oldenburg schools were closed, and we students were marched to the Landtag's Wiesen, the meadows surrounding the legislative buildings. When thousands were assembled, we heard a gentle humming in the air, growing ever louder. Floating directly above us, reaching across a massive arc of space, was a huge silvery mass, the airship LZ 129, the *Hindenburg*, named after our German president under Hitler. I was impressed by the ship's silent approach and that it could hover in the air and beam music and speech down on us. It was all new to me and at that age, I was unaware of the propaganda potential. The *Hindenburg's* celebrity ended within the year; after an uneventful transatlantic flight, the airship caught fire while attempting to dock in Lakehurst, New Jersey, on May 6, 1937. Instead of using nonflammable helium, the Zeppelin was filled with hydrogen, the same highly flammable substance that had caused my own test-tube explosions at home. The Nazi-controlled newspapers blamed the Lakehurst disaster on the American industry for refusing to export the nonflammable helium, a claim that did not make sense. The airship had been designed and constructed to be carried by hydrogen. The American industry had never been approached about helium beforehand nor were there any American backers. The Nazi press, however, who had presented the airship as a triumph of German technology, evaded responsibility for the disaster, which had cost thirty-six human lives.

The end of German hubris about air ship LZ 127, the Hindenburg, whose highly inflammable hydrogen was ignited by a spark on landing in Lakehurst, USA.

Our school assemblies turned more political after they were arranged and enforced by the increasingly powerful youth organization, the Hitler *Jugend*. Indoctrination, German national resurgence, and physical competition were stressed. To boost our respect for the new (and only) party, students were treated to a day off school for a free train journey to Bremerhaven, the deep sea harbour of the city of Bremen. The ocean liner *Bremen* was docked there and we were given the opportunity to tour the ship during an "open house" visit. I was impressed by the ship's enormous size. The *Bremen* carried a floatplane that could be lowered to the water by a crane. Loaded with mail for the United States, the aircraft would be launched hours before the ship's New York arrival and beat the regular overseas mail delivery time by nine hours. Early in World War II, the *Bremen* served as a barracks ship. Plans were to use her as a transport vessel in the intended invasion of Britain. However, in 1941 the vessel was set alight by a crew member while at her dock in Bremerhaven. As had the airship *Hindenburg* in 1937, so did the ocean liner *Bremen* become a victim of fire during the war.

Another unique opportunity for travel and exploration was offered to the schools of Oldenburg in form of a visit to Helgoland, an island in the German Bay. Originally owned and occupied by Britain, the place had a mystic and exotic patriotic past. The poet Hoffmann von Fallersleben, the creator of the German anthem, the *"Deutschland Lied,"* had been exiled from Prussia and Hannover for his revolutionary idea of a united Germany, and he took refuge on the British-occupied island. It was on Helgoland where he wrote the lyrics of the Deutschland song. An amnesty allowed his return home shortly. Helgoland became German property when Chancellor Bismarck acquired it from Great Britain in return for relinquishing a German monopoly on trade and commerce rights on the east African island of Zanzibar and neighbouring Uganda. Although with the Treaty of Versailles we had lost all of our colonies, Papua-New Guinea, the South Pacific archipelago, the territories in China, and the large areas in both East and West Africa, the Zanzibar-Helgoland deal seemed to have fallen through the cracks. Britain had not claimed the island back after World War I although Germany had fortified and used it as a base for submarine warfare. Helgoland had become a Nazi tourist destination, and visits were advertised in a popular, perhaps Party-inspired, song:

> *Kraft durch Freude fährt nach Helgoland*
> *Jeder Volksgenosse muss einmal zur See.*
> *Fünf Mark achtzig,*
> *Die Sache macht sich,*
> *Und den Rest bezahlt die NSDAP.*

Roughly translated, the organization *KdF, Kraft durch Freude* (Strength through Joy), was promoting a sea journey to Helgoland for every *Volks Fellow* at the ridiculously nominal price of 5.80 marks. It was understood that the

Party (acronym NSDAP, National Sozialistische Deutsche Arbeiter Partei) would make up for the balance. Under its minister Robert Ley, *KdF* seemed to be an altruistic creation of great ambition. Before being interrupted by the beginning of the war, construction of a huge resort for 30,000 was commenced on the Island of Rügen in the Baltic Sea. Two 25,000 ton cruise ships were completed and took *KdF* vacationers to exotic islands like Madeira, for the single-class fee of 120 marks. Mother agreed with my plan to visit Helgoland and was willing to release the six marks.

The plan for the journey to Helgoland coincided with the conclusion of the 1936 Olympic Games in Berlin. Ali Brockmann, the physical education teacher, had shown in the school gymnasium the film *Olympia*, produced by Hitler's favourite film maker, Leni Riefenstahl. We were enthralled with the new high-jump technique by which an American had cleared 2.03 metres. Using his take-off jumping leg also as the one on which he came down, the process involved easing his shoulders over the bar backward. At home, I imitated the method, jumping over a gooseberry bush in the garden, using the right leg for both taking-off and landing. I came down badly; the ankle was severely swollen; I could barely put weight on it and was confined to bed. In the absence of ice--we had no fridges then--Mother applied cold water compresses. It was the end of my Helgoland excursion and of my chance to gain Strength through Joy.

With three near-teenage boys on her hands, all growing, needing space in addition to food, clothes, and school textbooks, cooped up in an upstairs apartment, Mother could see that our accommodation was inadequate. She had the astuteness to look for a house as a permanent place to live, preferring to pay a mortgage rather than rent. Herr Oltmanns in Tweelbäke, a Methodist friend and previous neighbour, provided a loan of 17,000 marks, and we moved into a house, located on Bremer Strasse 27, in the city. It was an attractive classical style stuccoed brick house with vine-covered large decorative window shutters on the front, all at least one hundred years old. When I dug at the bottom of the foundation I uncovered a glazed earthen mug; my spade put a small chip in its rim. It is marked in Low German *een quartje*, one quart, probably dispensed and buried during the *Richt Fest* ceremony a century or more before. As for the loan on the house, Mother repaid the entire amount, plus interest, during the war at practically no sacrifice. It was not difficult; there were no other goods available, on which to spend money.

Now a property owner, she experienced the trials and advantages that came with her new status. In order to increase her income, she tersely advertised in the Oldenburger *Nachrichten*: "Room for Rent, including piano."

For Fräulein Edith Nischewski, a soprano opera singer and chorister from Nordhausen, who had obtained a position with the Oldenburg Staats Theatre, the location on Bremer Strasse 27 was ideal because of the five-minute walk to the theatre. The furnished room with our late father's Ibach piano came at the right price. She became Mother's long-standing tenant and financial support. Their friendship lasted through the war when together they put up with the collectors of imposed Nazi levies, house inspectors, party functionaries, and air wardens complaining of insufficient light-proofing. Mother, as a house owner and landlord, put up with bombing raids in which they all had to seek shelter in the cellar and, finally, the arrival of Canadian occupation troops. The tenant Miss Nischewski was not unattractive, extremely modest, and of temperate habits. She never brought any men home; we boys would have noticed immediately if she had. We could hear every word through the large double-winged door, which separated her room from our living room. I remember our tenant's soprano scale exercises, the chromatic variants of her do-re-mi-fa-sol solfaing and arias melding into a colourful musical potpourri during my homework of reciting Plato, Homer's *Iliad*, and Greek grammar and vocabulary.

The Nazi government had designated one Sunday of each month as an *Ein-Topf Sonntag,* a one-pot Sunday. The money saved by cooking a single-pot stew would allegedly go to the poor, and sharing a simple inexpensive meal would create solidarity. As the Nazis drove home that the Versailles Peace *Diktat* restricted the size of the German army severely, it was an open secret that the *Ein-Topf* program was a disguised contravention to finance German rearmament. To procure the *Ein-Topf* contribution of fifty pfennigs per family, the collector would call at noon, interrupting the main meal with the obligatory "Heil Hitler!" Mother would ridicule the system. Using a large ear trumpet, she would exaggerate her hearing difficulty and feign misunderstanding and ignorance: "Hitler?" She would shout in pretended confusion. "No, Hitler does not live here." In her disdain of the regime, Mother gambled with her freedom. Although she may have been brave, her profanation could have put us all in a concentration camp, if her blasphemy had been denounced.

In addition to Miss Nischewski, Mother had tenants upstairs in the attic apartment, the two Helms sisters, one of whom, Hertha, was a mongoloid, mentally and bodily impaired. Henni, the caring older sister, although rational, was stone deaf and, before the invention of electronic hearing aids, depended on a large hearing trumpet. They had lived upstairs for many years, using toilet buckets that were collected once a week by the "honey brigade" until Mother had the money to put in a flush water toilet for them. Henni took good care of her handicapped sister; she usually kept her indoors, in their apartment, for fear her impairment might become known. Unfortunately, however, her condition came to the attention of the Nazi health authority and according to a new law, she had to be taken to the hospital for sterilization. We suspected that the woman collecting the *Ein-Topf* fee had given her away. I learned later that the Gestapo drew eighty percent of their charges from denunciations by such fellow citizens. Although Henni was happy to have Hertha back from hospital, she knew that the same law also contained provisions empowering the State to place the unfortunate girl into an institution where people mysteriously died from some exotic horrible disease and were never seen again. Rumour had it that they were put to death by carbon monoxide. Henni Helms was careful about taking her sister out. Although having the Helms sisters augment Mother's widow's pension, we were still chronically short of money. On one occasion we did not have the twenty pfennigs handy to buy a needed exercise book for school.

All my years while in Oldenburg, I enjoyed the company and friendship of Georg Steinkamp, a person whom I met as the son of the church organist and our piano teacher. Georg was a highly gifted teenager, very musical, who was interested in everything that was going on—to me, a modern Renaissance man. His attitude towards life had a significant influence on my development. He was a devout Anglophile who had been to England at least once, by bike, staying in youth hostels. He told me how, on English roads, the grass was allowed to grow from the shoulder immediately to the paved surface without any gravel in between, an ideal setting for biking the countryside. He told me about Mount Snowdon, Wales' highest mountain, and the amusing pronunciation of the name of the Welsh town of Llandudno.

Georg always spoke about things nonchalantly, even if they were serious or dangerous, like Nazi politics. He told me the funny story about Hitler's visit to buy a new carpet for his office. Our Führer was known to be short-tempered, a trait which was often exaggerated as "throwing himself down in a tantrum and biting the carpet in a rage." So, when Hitler had made his choice of carpet, the salesman asked: "*Mein Führer*, do you wish me to wrap it up, or do you want to bite into it right here?"

Georg Steinkamp was a person whom we could trust as he shared our general dislike of the political exaggeration. Any of the Nazi restrictions, such as the law forbidding listening to foreign broadcasts, would induce him to do just that. On his visits, we would draw the curtains, make sure the front door was locked, and huddle in front of our radio. With the volume turned low, we would tune into the BBC from London. At the beginning of the war, we did not know which country was transmitting the facts although we trusted our own German version the least. The news was ambiguous and contradictory, and it became obvious that the hostilities had taken even to the the air waves. Often the British medium-wave transmission was drowned out by an eardrum-splitting noise; we knew that the jammer was our own government's, which did not want us to hear the truth. We would switch to the BBC's Long Wave Droitwich transmitter with its gigantic power output of over 100 kilowatts that reached us on 200 kilohertz without interference. It seemed like a cat-and-mouse game; the Russians jammed German broadcasts, and the Germans reciprocated. They blocked the BBC transmissions, and Britain probably jammed "Lord Haw Haw's" German propaganda broadcasts in English as well.

Doors locked, curtains drawn, volume low, these were our dire precautions when listening to the forbidden but more realistic and reliable BBC news.

The monthly fee for radio reception was two marks before and during the war. Initially, the amount was determined to be equal to the cost of sending a telegram abroad. In November, 1923, during the height of post-war inflation, the radio fee had been 35 billion marks; not many could afford the novelty.

Every time Georg invited me to his house, it became an adventure. The multitude of electric and mechanical gadgets in his room impressed me. He played to me on his saxophone, quite proficiently, preferring English songs such as "When the deep purple falls over sleepy garden walls and the stars begin to flicker in the sky, through the mist of my memory, you wander back to me, in the deep purple sky." George was an accomplished tap dancer; he introduced me to Buddy Ebsen's performance in the movie *Broadway Melody,* and even taught me some tap dancing.

Georg was a gymnast of high calibre and performed backward flips and somersaults from a standing position, usually in the summer on the soft sandy beach of our local Strand Bad. This was many years before gymnastics by twelve-year-old Olympic athletes became the rage. Adjacent to the legislative buildings in Oldenburg were the scenic Dobben Ponds, which were really a sewage lagoon for the city. On hot summer evenings, Georg and I went swimming there to cool off and, partly, to spite the commanding "Schwimmen Verboten" sign. Our bravado did us no harm although I would not go for a swim there now unless the reservoir has been rehabilitated, which it should be, located in the centre of a residential area.

The highlight of my relationship with Georg was our bicycle trip in Holland in 1938, one year before the war. Mother gave her consent immediately when she learned who my mentor was, although the timing to ask for money was inopportune. I had just gotten my way with her in our plan to buy a new radio, and a beauty it was, a Grundig super heterodyne receiver, our access to the outside world, away from Nazi propaganda, with three separate short-wave sections, and an input jack to play our 78 rpm shellac records of Beethoven symphonies over the speaker. At 250 marks, that luxury had cost her an arm and a leg, and modern financing with installments did not exist. However, the Holland tour would not affect her tight budget; we did not need to worry about buying foreign currency simply because customs regulations restricted us to the ridiculously low sum of forty-two marks to convert to Dutch guilders. I managed to hide an extra Dutch guilder coin in the knot of my necktie. Georg had the good idea to purchase train tickets in Germany to get us deep into Holland, to the farthest point we were going, Rotterdam, thus saving our valuable foreign funds for the return trip on our bikes.

Hubert Hamlin, American student of architecture at Princeton, was also a guest at the Rotterdam Youth Hostel.

Once in Rotterdam, we registered at the youth hostel. The guests were international; we met two Americans who had completed their tour and were about to ship home. They were anxious to talk with us. Georg had always encouraged my English studies and here was the first time I could apply my knowledge. One of the two, Hubert Hamlin, was an architecture student about to return home for his final examinations. We had good and profound conversations, including talks about Germany and Hitler. Discussing a possible war with Germany, he quoted the American president F. D. Roosevelt:

Gerd Asche

"I don't want war, Eleanor doesn't want war, James, Elliott, and Franklin do not want war; therefore, we shall not have war." I still have Hubert's photo. Strange as it seems, after the German invasion of Poland and the start of the hostilities, he wrote to me and spontaneously expressed his opinion that Germany's actions were justified, an obvious indication of his political naïveté. I am certain, he changed his opinion during the course of the war years into which he, no doubt, was also drawn.

While in Rotterdam, we visited a movie theatre playing the film *Alexander's Ragtime Band.* I well remember some of the soundtrack and how I enjoyed the rich vanilla ice cream wafers which, unlike in German movie theatres, were sold right in the aisles during the show. Our tour home through Holland was enjoyable. We met some good-natured hostility; kids called us *Duitse Muff*, recognizing our nationality by the different shape of our bike handlebars. We always stayed in youth hostels. I remember that at one, a converted old castle, the Kastell Assumburg at Heemskerk, we received cookies sprinkled with coloured sugar, called *Muisjes*, little mice, for free. It was the birthday of the Crown Princess Juliana, the later queen of the Netherlands.

At the Groningen Youth Hostel, Henk Scholtens, son of the hostel parents, took a parting picture of Georg Steinkamp and myself (far left) with his family and other guests.

Our last night in Holland we spent at the Groningen youth hostel where we met the son of the hostel parents, Henk Scholtens. Henk was an open-minded boy whom I thought to be above my level of intelligence. We wrote to each other until the beginning of the war when my being drafted precluded correspondence with foreign countries. Henk left an impression on me and, when I returned home at the conclusion of the war, one of my first questions to Mother was whether she had heard from Henk Scholtens. Henk was dead. He had met his maker when, probably in the spirit of enthusiasm for the New Order, he joined the Dutch SS, *Schutz Staffel,* the protective Nazi squadron. I do hope that his meeting us had not encouraged him to idolize everything German that to him may have been synonymous with the Nazi movement and may have led him to take the fatal step to join the SS. Certainly, neither Georg nor I ever praised the rascals. But when visiting abroad, we were in a situational schizophrenia. On the one hand, we were proud of the country from whence we came but on the other, we did not want to embellish or even defend its recent distasteful accomplishments. I do not know the details of Henk's demise. I would have liked to have kept him as a friend.

Here in Canada I have some good Dutch friends, some from near Groningen, but I have not inquired further about Henk. Perhaps I should feel a little guilty. Henk's unpropitious fatal step is an indication of the efficiency of Goebbels's propaganda machine, which reached beyond Germany's borders, jamming foreign radio transmissions and glorifying Nazi ideas among other nations. It had even impressed the American architecture student Hubert Hamlin.

Henk Scholtens fell victim to the persuasive Goebbels propaganda and enthusiastically joined the Netherland's Nazi SS.

As for my pathfinder and mentor Georg Steinkamp, I enjoyed the privilege of his friendship for more than eighty years. Exempted from military service during the war, he designed and manufactured optical instruments used for military visual reconnaissance. He became well-to-do later by his research in the field of ultrasound used to measure the density and assess the quality of solid material structures such as concrete bridge foundations and buildings. He lived in the city of Bremen, east of Oldenburg. I grieved with him over the loss of the bond he enjoyed with his wife Helga, a hospitable and charming lady, who suffers from progressive dementia. Unexpectedly, Georg passed away in April of 2011 at the age of 97.

Chapter 5

For as long as I can remember, Mother had subscribed to the Oldenburger *Nachrichten* as her source of daily news. After reading the paper, including the editorials by Dr. Kaiser, our neighbour, she would save the paper for wrapping things or, rather than spend money on bathroom tissue, would divide the pages into generous hand-sized sheets, which, when guests were expected, she would replace tactfully with a roll of softer, more socially acceptable material - she was carrying the social class burden of a country school principal's widow, mother of three high school students, competently.

One afternoon in November of 1938, the year I had cycled Holland with Georg Steinkamp, I came home from school and saw the *Nachrichten*, still undivided, on the kitchen table. I glanced at the headlines casually, expecting the usual propaganda not worth reading. This time, however, the front page grabbed my attention with news from Paris, that a German diplomat, vom Rath (the "vom" suggesting a provenance from German nobility) had been murdered by a German-Polish Jew named Grynspan. The murder left us cold; many of the aristocracy had jumped on the Nazi bandwagon. Was not Baldur von Schirach the new leader of the *Hitler Jugend*? Dr. Kaiser, who openly disliked Goebbels, was predicting that the information from Paris would provide a ripe plum to be picked by the Minister for Enlightenment and Propaganda, a known Jew hater. Indeed, Goebbels was quick to react, inflating the Paris trial into a public affair and claiming a Jewish conspiracy against German diplomats abroad. In response, supposedly-spontaneous anti-Jewish protests were organized. In Berlin, commandos started demolishing Jewish stores and desecrating places of worship in an orchestrated emotional reaction.

When our provincial town woke up to the news of the pogrom, it was a sensation that upset also the non-Jewish citizens. In Oldenburg, the synagogue was profaned, and store windows of Jewish-owned shops had been pillaged during the night. Even Mr. Kanz, our local butcher, had been targeted. Mother used to send us to him for ground meat for *Frikandellen* (meat balls), liver sausage, or the occasional tasty European wieners. We had a special relationship with him because he gave Mother credit until the beginning of the next month when her widow's cheque was due to arrive. That morning, Mother had gone herself to pick the right cut for a Sunday roast. She came home without meat. The little shop was closed; door and windows were smashed and nailed shut. Mr. Kanz was not there. We had not been aware, nor would we have cared, that the Kanzes were Jewish. Herr Kanz never appeared again and Mother, as she would remain silent at the disappearance of Dr. Kaiser, prudently kept from asking about him. The shop reopened later under Frau Kanz, an "Aryan," and Mother's credit was still good.

In addition to the butcher and other victims whom we did not know, two of our Gymnasium classmates, Löwenstein and Goldschmidt, who had taken optional Hebrew language instruction, remained ominously absent; their seats were assigned to other students, and the teaching of Hebrew was taken off the school's curriculum. About their absence we could not inquire, but we were curious to see for ourselves the visible results of the night's vandalism. Yet the usual spectators, such as those who might be attracted to look at a house after a fire or an accident, remained notably absent; Peter Street in front of the synagogue was empty of people. We dared not go; our interest might be taken as disapproval of the action or as an expression of sympathy with the victims. We found our own way to bear witness.

A classmate who had access to his dad's Pentax 35 mm camera, Justin Hüppe, enjoyed taking pictures. He was notorious for his surreptitious photographs of our teachers while they taught in class. Justin decided that he was going to photograph the damage. His friend Inge Tebbe was the daughter of the director of the Children's Hospital which was right across the street from the synagogue. Dr. Tebbe who, as a Catholic, was more anti-Nazi than many of the local Protestants, gave us permission to enter, and Justin led us inside the hospital. Using a telephoto lens, he took photographs of the willful destruction through the window of the glass door. As we surveyed the brutal ransack, we realized that what had happened to the Jews could happen to any of us.

Our neighbour Dr. Kaiser, editor of the Oldenburger *Nachrichten*, who predicted how the murder in Paris would be exploited by the Nazi Party in Germany, routinely published anti-Nazi editorials, which were impressive and to the point. I learned that he had been taken into "*Schutz Haft*," so-called protective custody, an ironic term for depriving him of his freedom. The only protection he needed was from those who had arrested him. Afraid that showing our sympathy might be seen as a political expression, we neighbours and previous friends of the Kaiser family kept our distance and, as we had with the disappearance of Herr Kanz, refrained from demonstrating our compassion.

Contrary to Goebbels' intention, the barbarity of the attacks did arouse feelings of sympathy for these people, our marked neighbours. That night of November 9 to 10 became known by Goebbels' phrase as Kristallnacht (crystal night), deliberately evoking the idea of crystal chandeliers, cut glass wine goblets, fine table cloths and silver, or precision instruments and watches. The propagandist was attempting to impress that the action was spontaneous, civilized, and committed by refined, sophisticated, reasonable, upper-class people. But it was widely known that the attacks were not the desperate reaction of cultivated Germans outraged at a perceived Jewish conspiracy, and the vandalism became an embarrassment to Goebbels when more light was shed on the motive for the diplomat's murder.

Originally, the assassin of vom Rath was said to have been distraught because his German Jewish family had been forcibly removed to Poland. Then the news leaked out that the murder in Paris had been the result of a lovers' quarrel, a murder of passion, of jealousy in a homosexual relationship between vom Rath and Grynspan. Goebbels had heard the second version at the last moment and had attempted to call off the SA and SS-organized demonstrations, to cancel the press coverage which had already been arranged, but it was too late. There had been no time for "Back now, broom, into the closet!" His attempt to ascribe the violence to spontaneous indignation of the German people driven to react to Jewish behaviour was recognized as subterfuge, utter nonsense. Of course, the Jews had not misbehaved; neither would we dream of damaging the property of others, Jewish or "Aryans," but no one dared speak out in protest, lest he or she would be labelled an anti-Nazi, an enemy of the State. Goebbels' version of *Kristallnacht* may have convinced observers in foreign countries where there was freedom of speech, to accept the claim that the action with the refined name was executed justifiably by reasonable citizens. We, inside Germany, knew better but did not dare to publicize the truth.

Kristallnacht marked the beginning. We felt indignant about the conduct of the hoodlums. But the Nazis themselves were a different class from the vandals; they were unpredictable; they had the power to do to any of us whatever they pleased. We became extra careful, wary, and silent, in some cases fearful. Herr Kanz had disappeared that night and never returned. And Dr. Kaiser, whose editorials had resulted in his being placed into "protective custody," also paid the price for defending freedom of expression. I learned many years later, from his son and daughter, Bodo and Edeltraut, when they visited Vancouver, that their father had died miserably in the concentration camp.

The Führer forgave his propaganda minister's *Kristallnacht* slip-up. There were greater issues at stake. The gossip trickled through that under the pretence of preparing to film a movie, SS-organized German military operatives, wearing Polish uniforms, had attacked a German radio station in the border town of Gleiwitz. As Georg Steinkamp and I heard during our secret listening-in on August 31, the BBC announced: "*There have been reports of an attack on a radio station in Gleiwitz, which is just across the Polish border in Silesia. The German News Agency reports that the attack came at about 8:00 p.m. this evening when the Poles forced their way into the studio and began broadcasting a statement in Polish. Within a quarter of an hour,*" the report said, "*the Poles were overpowered by German police who opened fire on them. Several of the Poles were reported killed, but the numbers are not yet known.*"

This was the German-staged *agent-provocateur* operation that Hitler used as a *pro forma* reason when on September 1,1939, German troops swarmed across the Polish border and unleashed the first Blitzkrieg. Poland's defense was prepared for the long outdated World War I warfare. As a result, their well-trained cavalry on horses was useless against the steel of German tanks. Two days later, at 11:00 a.m., I tuned in to the BBC and heard Prime Minister Chamberlain announce that a state of war now existed between Great Britain and Germany. It was common knowledge that the attack on Radio Gleiwitz was phony, staged by Germans in Polish disguise to create a reason for invading Poland. The consequences were only too real—the staged show initiated World War II.

Chapter 6

Although Hitler knew well that both France and England had issued a guarantee to protect the integrity of Poland, he was gambling to get away with the invasion of Poland, counting on the weakness and indecision of France's premier Daladier and Britain's Chamberlain, ridiculed for using his umbrella for a walking stick. Hitler had already succeeded in his occupation of Czechoslovakia, despite Premier Chamberlain's personal appeal for peace. If the invasion should lead to a war, however, Hitler was well prepared for a larger conflict. In the end, *Der Führer* had miscalculated this time; the allies declared war within twenty-four hours. World War II had begun.

School is over. Oh, what fun! Knickerbockers, down to mid-calf, were in fashion. Litlle did I expect to find at home a brown letter that drafted me into the government Labour Service.

The pre-war atmosphere affected us at the school. We were the class scheduled to graduate at the end of the year. My photographer friend Justin Hüppe decided to record our class coherence in a few happy pictures since we might never again be able to enjoy each other's friendship.

Our graduating class "cabbage party."

During our senior class "cabbage party" at the Waldhaus Restaurant, classmate Peter Modick's placard boldly displayed the mock resolution to keep guzzling the suds. It was an afternoon of harmless fun, a good meal with all the kale you could eat, and two beers, all at the price of one mark per person. About to be free from the yoke of school, our exuberant class would soon face the raw awakening of military life in war.

The Class of 1939, Oldenburg Gymnasium.

Helmuth Röver, fifth from the left, wore a military uniform; he had already been drafted into the air force. At war's end, many would no longer be alive. Seventy-five years later, the class had dwindled to four, Siems, wearing glasses, kneeling at the far left, Wichmann, kneeling, third from left, Fehlhaber kneeling, fifth in the row, and me, Asche, standing in the top row, far right, with my left hand in the pocket.

Four old fellows, survivors after seventy-five years.
We are but few and met recently over a beer.

As early as July 1939, there had been proof of Germany's war preparations. Weeks before the incident at the Gleiwitz radio station, while it was still peace time, and I had completed my last year at the Gymnasium, the Hitler Youth had commandeered the entire school to the task of picking the potato fields for the well-known black and yellow-striped potato beetles. Upon my return from the country, a brown government letter awaited me at home. The missive had significant bearing on my immediate future, putting an abrupt end to the completion of my studies and my carefree school life. I was drafted into the *Reichs Arbeits Dienst* (RAD), the quasi-military government labour service. The conscription of school boys and students from their benches and interrupting their education was indicative of an unusual military manpower shortage, as if the country were in a state of national emergency. And yet, there was no war, no obvious cause for this extraordinary measure until our eyes were opened by the September invasion against the "uprising" Poles. War had been secretly planned, the invasion of Poland pre-conceived, starting with the drafting of students, and followed by the staged Gleiwitz incident.

A directive from the Ministry of Education mitigated the abruptness of my draft order. Those students whose secondary education was interrupted by their recruitment, were deemed to have attained high school maturity, to have passed their *abitur* finals without examination and be eligible for university admission. Thus, becoming a worker, a labourer of the RAD, paradoxically elevated me to a semi-academic status. Admittedly, my scholastic standing was atrocious, and I might have failed if I had had to submit to the examinations. Like it or not, I temporarily benefited from the pre-war situation as practically all Germans did, one way or another. Although my university eligibility would be irrelevant until any hostilities were over and I was released, the rapid developments—the recent re-occupation of the Rhineland, the annexation of Czechoslovakia, the Blitzkrieg against Poland and its partition with Russia, and the invasions of Norway, Holland, Belgium, and France—made us believe that a war would not last long, and we soon could count on enrolling at the universities, or so we thought. In retrospect, conferring unearned academic privileges in return for military enlistment was an irresponsible measure; the level of scientific education and progress in Germany would be set back for a generation.

Gerd Asche

Arbeits Dienst **boot camp with pre-military drill, using the spade instead of the rifle. I stand number three in the front row.**

I was in good physical condition when I entered the *Arbeits Dienst* through one of their boot camps. The exercise and the drill with the spade (in lieu of the rifle and in preparation for military service) agreed with me. I made the best of an inconvenient situation and was promoted to *Vor Mann*, foreman, which to me meant a little more pay. Since the *Wehrmacht,* the German armed forces, had already conquered France, Belgium, Norway, and Holland, our unit was transferred from our camp near Hamburg directly to France, to a small unknown seaside town at Cap Gris Nez on the channel coast in the Pas de Calais region. On our way, I had the opportunity to visit the cemetery of the German soldiers who had recently lost their lives in the Battle of Dunkirk that was hailed as a great military success and deceivingly referred to as the Second Battle of Waterloo, although the distribution of forces was nearly the opposite 125 years before, with Prussia's Marshal Blücher and Britain's General Wellington defeating France's Emperor Napoleon. It was the first time I encountered a mass of fresh military graves and the custom to top the grave crosses with the soldiers' steel helmets. This ceremonial observance would soon be reduced to the planting of wooden crosses alone; there was a shortage of steel helmets. We had been told nothing of the valiant withdrawal by the British and Canadians. German history still likes to self-assertively dwell on the 1815 battle of nearby Waterloo, the importance of and dependence on Prussian troops in

Wellington's quoting impatiently: "I wish it were nighttime, or Blücher would arrive."

Graves of German soldiers killed in the Battle of Dunkirk early in the war. The ritual of topping each cross with a helmet was later abandoned; there were not enough steel helmets to go around.

Historically, our destination in France, the town of Wimereux, was the location of the British General Headquarters of the British Army during World War I. Again, during World War II, the British Rear Headquarters was forced to retreat from Boulogne to Wimereux for a few days in May, 1940, until the British Expeditionary Force was expelled completely, and the town was in German hands. Our unit ended up in Wimereux as our quarters for military work at nearby Cap Gris Nez. We were assigned a previous bed-and-breakfast place called *La Chaloupe*. On moving into our room, I noted that the British had hastily vacated the place a few days earlier. As I lifted the mattress of my bed, I found a sleeping bag, left behind by its previous occupant, probably a British officer. The material was of fine quality, natural silk, and bore a small label, "Ducks of Greenock." Weighing less than one pound and compressible to a small size, yet extremely well insulating when used outdoors, this booty served me well throughout the war and is now stored in our attic in Hope.

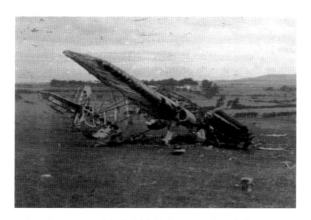

A sad memento of the brief British occupation of Wimereux and what was left behind before their evacuation via Dunkirk.

Payday in Wimereux, France, receiving German occupation money where Pound Sterling ruled a few days ago.

It was only recently, many years after I had immigrated, when I became aware of Canada's national and cultural ties to this insignificant town on the Channel coast. Watching the CBC documentary *In Flanders Fields*, I learned of our link to the little resort town in northern France and the reason for the unusual name of one of its streets, *Rue du* Colonel *McCrae*. The Canadian doctor, Lieutenant-Colonel John McCrae, creator of the stirring poem of the Great War, lies buried in the local cemetery after his death on January 18, 1918.

We are the Dead. Short days ago
We lived, felt dawn, saw sunset glow,
Loved and were loved, and now we lie
In Flanders fields.

La Chaloupe (listed on the Internet as back in business again, catering mostly to British tourists) was located directly on the beach. In the morning, trucks would take us to the work site on Cap Gris Nez, the dunes directly on the shore closest to the coast of England. We had to erect six giant masts; the place was to be the location of the *Knickebein* (crooked leg, name of liquor-filled chocolate Easter eggs) *Peilung*, an electronic beaming device to guide the German bombers to London at night, only a hundred miles away. Once over the target, the formations would receive a coordinating cross-signal across the North Sea, from another beam on the Norwegian coast, indicating the moment to release their sinister cargo. It was ironic to see a memorial tablet indicating that from this very location of our gigantic radio structure Marconi had made his first peacetime radio contact from France to England on May 28, 1899.

A distant view of our workplace, Cap Gris Nez, the spot closest to England.

We helped erect masts for the radio beam system, code name Knickebein.

On our way to work, our truck would pass through a marble quarry near the town of Marquise, a high security no-stop zone where road signs and the *Feld Polizei* forced vehicles to keep moving. I noticed passing a huge structure, a tunnel built of solid concrete, several hundred feet long. There was talk that this site was the location of a large retractable super gun to fire missiles, nine feet long, at London. Was this one of Hitler's announced secret V-weapons, the "V" inferring *Vergeltung*, vengeance? Although we did not know what was to be revenged, we realized that if it concerned the bombing of civilians, the Germans certainly had the lead; was I not, with my own hands, contributing to the installation of the *Knickebein* guidance system to lead the German bombers to London as early as 1940? The secrecy about the site was tantalizing; from the back of the moving shaky truck I was able to obtain a photographic glimpse of the structure; the poor quality of the picture reflects the difficulty and precautions I took to obtain it.

The giant bunker tunnel said to contain one of Germany's secret V-weapons.

I did not have to work very hard in the dunes; there was time and opportunity to look at the British coast through a military "scissors" telescope. On a clear day, the chalky white cliffs of England and the barrage balloons that prevented attacks by low-flying enemy planes were visible over Folkestone. From across the Channel we could hear the rumbling when the British fired their anti-aircraft guns, or was it the detonation of German bombs and the V-weapons?

Lunch break in the dunes of Cap Gris Nez. My mess kit is lying on the ground next to me.

Taking a peek at the English coast, the white cliffs of Dover.

For our next work project, we were transferred from Wimereux to the nearby town of Marquise where our unit came into contact with the local French people. Here the Gymnasium-acquired French of Dr. Naumann put me in good stead. Because of the excellent pronunciation upon which he had always insisted, I became the official inter- preter overnight. Excused from labour and drill, I made purchases and arranged services for our unit. This appoint- ment not only boosted my French language skills, it also provided more contact with the local, albeit politely hostile, population. We stayed in a schoolhouse and enjoyed our less restricted freedom.

One of our work assignments was to extend and level off a Luftwaffe landing strip for Messerschmidt 109 fighters. Because of their short flying range, the planes would join the bombers at the last moment, from the French shoreline, to protect them on their way across the Channel. I suppose there were some aces among the pilots but they had no interest in us lowly workmen except that our work extending the runway offered them a safer landing. After the fighters returned from a cross-Channel operation, German Luftwaffe high brass would arrive for debriefing. Instead of the oppor- tunity to fraternize with one of the celebrated aviator aces, I had to be content to have a friend take my picture with his fighter plane that showed a "decoration" of eight bars painted on the plane's rudder, indicating eight witnessed kills. While the distinction demonstrated evidence of the pilot's skill and success in the air, it conveyed to me eight unknown tragedies and sorrows caused on the other side.

Air war against England. After the fighters returned from a cross-Channel operation, the German Luftwaffe high brass arrived for debriefing.

Eight victories in the air earned Hitler's Knight's Cross, at the price of eight grieving families elsewhere.

Since our quarters were adjacent to the Channel beach, we witnessed enemy fighter aircraft making emergency landings on its smooth but soft surface. While the German pilots knew of the nearby landing strip we had improved for them, the British fighter pilots saw their only possibility to land by crashing their aircraft on the unstable sand beaches.

Out of fuel, the pilot of this allied fighter could not make it home and chose a German POW camp over ditching in the icy grave of the Channel.

The intensity of Goebbels' Nazi propaganda increased during the war. The most effective dissemination of news was by radio broadcast, and the government had designed a special *Volks Empfänger*, an affordable regenerative radio receiver, sensitive enough for local stations but unsuitable for foreign broadcasts. To prime the listeners for favourable news and the expected victory, the *Wehrmacht Berichts*, the broadcast announcements from the front, were ushered in by a special musical theme. Although one would have expected a melody by the Führer's favourite composer, Richard Wagner, it was music by a no-less famous Hungarian friend of Wagner's which cued the listeners to expect victory-- the heraldic fanfare motif of the *March Finale* from Franz Liszt's *Preludes*.

A prelude indeed was my six-month compulsory *Arbeits Dienst* service. When I came home, there was another brown government envelope awaiting me; it contained an order to report for military enlistment.

Chapter 7

Two weeks at home and freedom from military discipline of the Arbeits Dienst were disappointing; my friends and acquaintances had also been drafted. When I duly reported to the *Pferdemarkt Kaserne*, Oldenburg's Horse Market barracks, my record of previous experience in electronics and communications must have impressed the recruiting clerk. He assigned me to the army signals branch in Hamburg for a six-week recruit training which I had no trouble surviving. In fact, during target practice, each of my three shots hit the bull's-eye, earning me a sharpshooter's three-day pass. While at home on leave, Mother insisted that we three have our photograph taken. Father's experience had taught her the devastating effect a war can have on what is left of a family. The picture speaks the trite "thousand words," contrasting the carefree and happy three brothers of a few years earlier during peacetime, with the sombre faces of youths expecting to become cannon fodder.

The three young Asche brothers, carefree and happy.

Three brothers, sombre in the light of the coming conscription, with one drafted and two more to go.

My further training included a transfer from Hamburg to a technical school in Halle on the Saale River to become familiar with basic electronics and communications. We learned the principle of *Träger Frequenz* (TF) transmission, a technique by which multiple channels of communication are modulated onto individual radio frequencies. However, rather than broadcast the signals as radio stations do, TF feeds the conversations to a discreet telephone line. At the receiving end, a corresponding modem would separate the arriving channels and demodulate the signals into audible speech. By this means, it was possible to transmit twenty-eight channels, either telephone conversations or teleprints simultaneously over two simple telephone wires, an ideal mode of communication for mobile warfare at the time.

**At the conclusion of the TF course I was allowed to
take the picture of the successful graduates.**

As a precaution against espionage and interception, to
prevent the straying of secret information, of enemy jamming,
induction of external inadvertent electrical noises (such as
hash, hum, other signals, or atmospheric interference), the
two regular copper-clad steel wires were strung on poles
along the axis of an advancing army in a special configuration, arranged in a spiral pattern, called *Dreh Schleife*, rota-
tory loop, comparable to the more recent description of a
DNA double helix configuration. The wires were first attached
to one telephone pole on the left and right, to the next pole
both on the same side, one insulator above the other, to the
third pole again horizontally, but this time it was right above
left, and so forth, to form a continuous spiral for hundreds of
kilometres. The advantage was simplicity and the extremely
quick provision of and reliable communication with a fast
moving, advancing army, the requirement for a successful
Blitzkrieg. To the traditional frontline supply of trucks, loaded
with weapons, ammunition, fuel, or food, were added lorries
with telephone poles, spools of wire, insulators, and construction crews stringing the lines along the advance road,
even while fighting was still going on. It was the beginning
of a change from open warfare to one dependent upon and
controlled via electronic wire communications.

Gerd Asche

Thus, our *Träger Frequenz* 1 (TF1 company), the first of the *Wehrmacht's* three such units, was ideal for the provision of reliable communication between the troops advancing quickly at the front and the switchboard in the *Wolf's Schanze* (Wolf's Lair), Hitler's headquarters. The information would safely, instantly, travel over a thousand kilometres to the Führer Bunker concealed somewhere near Rastenburg in East Prussia. Signal attenuation (loss of strength over distance) was compensated by amplifier stations boosting the transmissions about every fifty to one hundred kilometres. The maintenance of these spiraling rotating-loop connections, the communications link for the advancing army, was a vital military necessity. Some booster stations were manned by specialists, equipped with delicate instruments, to locate faults by intricate techniques. An efficient fault locator like technician Theo Rapp could pinpoint a broken wire or a "short" with fair accuracy from a distance of fifty kilometres and would dispatch and summon a repair crew stationed near the place of interruption. Alternate means of communicating through local telephone lines or wireless were too unreliable for the modern warfare of the 1940s.

Alarm! The connection to Hitler's *Wolf Schanze* HQ in Germany is down! Theo Rapp has completed his Varley calculations, locating a line break, 123 kilometres east. He will summon the area repair crew.

Hitler had assigned the conquest of Leningrad, code-named Barbarossa (after the mythical name of an ancient German emperor), to General von Leeb, commander of Army Group North, and our TF1 Company was to support that operation. A second company, TF2, was serving Army Group Centre in their task to take Moscow, and a third unit, TF3, was in training to facilitate the conquest of Southern Russia by Army Group South. For his opening attack on northern Russia, General von Leeb had moved his divisions to the eastern border of East Prussia as a staging point. Our company had settled in a small village in the vicinity, close to the frontier with Russian-occupied Lithuania. On June 22, we received marching orders to cross the border the next morning. Each of us was given with his ration a bottle of Rhine wine, a truly rare allotment, indicating the significance of the undertaking. I remember that occasion well because it happened to be the day before my birthday.

The next morning, we crossed the border without incident. Fully motorized and able to be operative within an hour, we communications technicians were carefully kept away from combat, but following behind, close to the advancing army group. There was no enemy resistance; we felt as if we were on a holiday adventure, when our column stopped briefly at the Lithuanian town of Pilviskaia. Our company commander dispatched a group of three to search for gasoline. They returned shortly, without fuel, although they had apprehended an injured escaped Russian soldier whom they proudly took prisoner.

Discovering the Russian soldier hidden in a basement in Pilviskaia, Lithuania, Erich Peters, Theo Rapp, and George Muth bandaged his injured arm and took him prisoner.

The campaign had started late. To bring it to an end before winter, the move east was hasty. The fast advance caused confusion, errors, and accidents. Our motorized unit included motorcycles with a sidecar attached, used to carry messages or personnel from the front of the moving column to the rear. One such bike was operated by Erich Peters who felt that the best protection against enemy attacks was to travel close behind a heavy tank, in this case the hulk of a German Panzer. When the tank stopped during a traffic hold-up, the motorbike pulled up directly behind the monster, its front wheel almost touching the track. Unexpectedly, the impatient tank commander decided to bypass the traffic jam by shearing-out and advancing across the open field. Making a sharp right turn with the giant vehicle involved engaging the left tracks to move forward and the right tracks into reverse. As the tank lurched, it struck the bike behind it. Erich, the bike driver, got off in time and survived but was unable to push his vehicle with the passenger sidecar out of the way. Its occupant was crushed to death. This avoidable accident, the first fatality of our company's operation, shocked us as if we had lost a family member.

What place could be safer, Erich Peters thought, than driving his motorbike with a sidecar passenger close behind a T3 tank?

We pushed the now useless bike off the road and, minus one TF technician, continued to follow the column. During a short stop, we saw a burned-out Russian tank on the roadside. I strolled over for an inspection, climbed up, lifted the cover, and saw that the driver was still inside, dead. Still holding on to the controls, he was completely naked, his clothes burned off. What struck me, looking straight at me, was his penis. The organ had been well preserved against the flash fire by the muscles of his thighs and was sticking out perversely, facing me provocatively, as though still alive. I advised Lieutenant Holtmann to take a look also. Thus, the Russian tank driver trapped in his steel sarcophagus and the German TF soldier crushed to death in a motorcycle sidecar were the first two casualties on my birthday, the first morning of the Russian Campaign. We resumed our journey in a sepulchral spirit, unaware of the surprises the rest of the remarkable day might have in store.

The Lieutenant climbed up, lifted the cover, took a look, and called it a Russian soldier's steel sarcophagus.

Our advance continued without interruption; we reached the city of Kovno in Lithuania an hour later, sharp on the heels of *Armee Gruppe Nord*. The main bridge across the Nemen (Memel) River was down and we entered the residential area via a detour over a pontoon bridge. For quarters we were assigned a villa with all amenities, furniture, beds, clothes in the wardrobes, even food left on the table, a pleasant place with a view of the city and the Kovno synagogue. Judging by the quality of their appurtenances, the owners were well-to-do people, cultured intellectuals, and better off than my own family as I could tell from the furniture, the fine material of their suits, and their Lithuanian, Russian, and German library. One book was Hermann Sudermann's familiar *Litauische Geschichten* (*Stories of Lithuania*) that I remembered as one among my father's favourites. However, the assumed hospitality was deceptive as we could soon tell that the villa had been vacated in a great rush. These people must have left against their will, unexpectedly, and under most cruel conditions. The more I thought, the more I became concerned. Indeed, we found that we were occupying a Jewish residence.

Approaching the Lithuanian town of Kovno, the bridge across the Nemen River was down, and we reached the town by a detour and pontoon bridge.

The quarters we were assigned were very comfortable, with a view of the city and the nearby synagogue.

I did not have time to give much thought to the fate of the previous occupants. While we were settling in, assigning the beds and spreading our blankets, there was a call for me to report to the lieutenant. He had taken up the master bedroom of the house and was occupied with the parking, servicing,

Gerd Asche

and security of our special vehicles, but I noted that the loss of one of his men in the collision with the tank was bearing hard on him. He was upset and confessed: "I should write to the parents now, Asche, but I am too busy and want you to draft the letter for me." Lt. Holtmann had received his schooling in Bielefeld, Westphalia, to Grade Seven, when he became a carpenter in his father's small furniture factory. However, the war industry converted the family enterprise into producing aluminum mess kits and field flasks, and the son changed careers, becoming a professional military officer now commanding our TF Company. He was aware of my more complete education. Although his literary request was unexpected, there was no shortage of timely expressions; after all, we had been at war for over a year. I recalled from memory the newspaper obituaries for fallen soldiers and their keywords: fatherland, führer, field of honour, heroic, valiant, missed by his comrades. Using a plethora of suitable platitudes, I created a letter of condolence. When I submitted my composition to him, Lt. Holtmann signed it and had me take it to the *Feld Post.*

I had barely settled in, when there was another call from him: "The division bakery has been unable to keep up with us; it will probably be tomorrow before they get across the river and we can get their bread. Use my car and have Erich Peters, the driver, take you around town to find some bread for the company for tonight." Bread? How? Should I look up "Bread" in the phone book? Why did the lieutenant pick on me, a private? Would he not get better results from his sergeant major or the other NCOs? We set out on the quest and found the people friendly and very helpful, happy to be liberated from the dreaded Russians. We called on the bakeries without success; there was no bread to be had; stores and market stalls had run out of food.

The shortage of bread would soon extend to other foodstuff as well. Public market stalls were empty, devoid of victuals.

On our search, we passed a crowd in the forecourt of a gasoline station and stopped to inquire. A group of about twenty men stood there, in proper attire, some wearing neckties, their trousers creased, their shoes polished, kept under guard by civilians wearing some armbands, obviously fellow Lithuanians. The prisoners were herded together and lined up in a queue, guarded by a thug who was openly relieving himself. A young man--he must have been a Lithuanian also--was armed with an iron pipe. He commanded one of the men from the line-up to step forward, and in broad daylight and full view of the assembled crowd and quite coldly, struck the victim over the head. When the man was down, he beat him mercilessly until he was dead.

Guarded from the rear against escape, facing certain death, what may have been the last thoughts of those twenty waiting in line?

The onlookers appeared to condone the brutality; some even applauded as one would encourage an actor's performance, when it was the next prisoner's turn to step forward. Before them on the ground lay about twenty bodies in puddles of dark fluid. Guarded from the rear against escape and facing certain death, the twenty waited in line. While I was standing there amongst the crowd, I heard a deep agonized groan emerge from one of the bodies in front of me. The executioner heard this also; he turned and, in a frantic, fanatic manner, began beating the body again. I can still hear the dull drumming thud of the heavy pipe striking, cracking the ribs inside the chest cavity. When there was quiet, he made the next man in line step up. The dark puddles between the corpses strewn on the ground were blood; the rest of the yard was flooded with water.

Turned on by groaning from one of the bodies, the killer silenced it with his crow bar.

The victims, we learned, were local Jews. Were these perhaps the very people who owned the apartment whose comforts we were usurping and enjoying now? Although we never spoke about it, I knew that my companion Erich shared my feeling of guilt, wondering what those awaiting their turn had been thinking. It was a brutal massacre carried out by an inhumane thug of the lowest order, under the indulgence or at least the tacit approval of the German SS military supervision. It was a singularly horrendous crime; nobody, no matter how heinous the offence, deserves to be treated that way. Of the spectators, no one in his right mind would stay. We drove off. The scene has been with me ever since. I have never spoken about it to anyone, and Erich never discussed the experience with me or with our superior. I would know because if he had, the lieutenant would have called me to give an account, and I feel relieved to be finally able to share the load of this experience with the reader.

Repulsed by the cruel show, Erich and I returned to our quarters without a crumb of bread. There was no marching order for the next day, and we were more successful in our search for victuals. We drove past the fortress buildings of Kovno where a lot of men and women were held, perhaps people like those who had been made to vacate their apartment, presumably Jewish. Two nice-looking girls of my own age were among a group confined behind an iron fence; they caught my attention, beckoning to me, as any person in distress would. "Had I any idea what would happen to them, where they were going?" Before the war, I had heard of "resettlement" of undesirables and of concentration camps but could not imagine these two girls to be candidates; they looked and acted like any girl, spoke German like I did, and were modest and well behaved. I had an idea, though, of their being transported somewhere, in closed freight cars, perhaps causing them inconvenience, as we ourselves had endured on previous relocations by rail. I had not heard of the death camps and was polite as one would be to people of one's own, if not of a higher social station, and although I feared an ominous future for the girls, I tried to comfort and assure them.

To bring the campaign to an end before winter, the move east was planned and carried out in haste. Although the Kovno carnage will remain indelible in my memory, new events kept us too busy to have the massacre occupy our conscience for long. Our crews, following close behind the advancing vehicles, were erecting telephone poles and stringing wires to secure instant communication. Every fifty kilometres or so, along the completed TF line, maintenance posts were installed for speedy repair of the vital link, should a fault in the line occur. These faults were mostly weather-induced; acts of sabotage were not a factor as long as the German civil administration remained reasonable and appeared humane.

We were well equipped to locate these faults directly from the main station. Our tools were the electric principles of the Wheatstone bridge in the modification of the "Murray Loop." We corroborated our measurements by the "Three Varley Method," requiring multiple readings of the various resistance combinations of the faulted conductor with the aid of intact lines if they could be utilized. By subtraction and division of numbers, using the ratio of resistance from the point of measurement to the fault, we could obtain the distance to the defect by multiplying the figure with the total length of the line and eliminate some of the inaccuracies of the "Murray Loop" modality. The "Three Varley Method" must be performed by a trained operator as several measurements and computations are required. Calculators or computers, tape recorders, nickel-cadmium batteries, coaxial cable, fibre-optic lines, light-emitting diodes, global positioning satellites or other means of spatial determination were unknown seventy years ago; we depended on the use of the slide ruler and paper and pencil. Additional training distinguished us as fault locators from the regular technical TF crew, even from our military superiors, and we arrogantly considered ourselves more sophisticated and intellectually above most officers until the drills twice a week put us in our place again, a peg or nine down on the ladder of military rank and file.

A day after we had arrived in the Russian town of Pskow, a call came for me to report to Lt. Holtmann. I recalled the recent request for letter-writing to the mother of one of my deceased comrades, the assignment to procure bread for our unit, and coming across the blood bath in the yard of the Kovno service station on the afternoon of my birthday. What exotic order would await me this time? I stood at attention before the lieutenant and one of his brother officers. The lieutenant approached me, shook my hand, and congratulated me on the occasion of my birthday. He obviously was unaware of the slaughter I had witnessed on the previous day. From a bottle he poured a glassful of strong Russian vodka and handed it to me with the order to drink up. In the presence of another company commander, I felt obliged to carry out the order, demonstrating a sort of fealty to my lieutenant, and I managed to empty the glass. The incident seemed to be significant since it was photographed without my knowledge. Perhaps I was a pawn in a contest between two officers competing about their men's loyalty and obedience; perhaps it was a form of hazing since I had just reached the age of twenty-one. Understandably, I do not recall the results of the initiation except for a life-long dislike of vodka, a distaste amplified by the arrival of caseloads of vodka when vital nourishment, bread, was unavailable.

Called before the Lieutenant for a belated birthday congratulations, on my coming-of-age at twenty-one, I complied with his order to finish the glass of hundred-proof vodka.

The season changed; October had come to the aid of the enemy. Our troops lacked winter clothing; the German trucks and tanks had not been winterized, and their summer tires became mired in the mud of the Russian swamps. According to the plan, the war in the north should have been over. However, the army had advanced only as far as Lake Ladoga; our TF Company, kept back from the front, settled for the winter near the city of Pskow, Pleskau, where our equipment and quarters occupied several log buildings that were part of a vacated college or university complex. We had a lot of free time on our hands, and one ingenious fellow had procured the human skeleton left from anatomy class and arranged by string and pulleys and a protruding broomstick that whenever the door next to it was opened, the bony structure would go through an obscene motion. While the tasteless artistry seemed clever, it demonstrated how little our TF Company was involved in the life-and-death struggle of the two countries and their soldiers dying in the trenches every day. It also showed the blunting of esteem for human life and dignity.

The vulgar skeletal contraption was out of place and only existed for a few days because the room was set up as a more permanent station for the twenty-eight channels of communication to the *Wolf's Schanze* switchboard in East Prussia. For occasional diversion, trucks would take us to town to see a German movie or some other entertainment. The road led past a huge fenced-in area, a Russian prisoner-of-war camp. A low-level moaning and groaning wafted from behind the barbed wire. These men were dying; they had no food. Some prisoners were still standing to keep warm--they had nothing with which to keep a fire going--but most were sitting or lying on the bare frozen ground to die. Their starvation was not planned cruelty; there simply was no food for a hundred thousand.

En route from our workplace outside of the city of Pskow to see a German show, we passed a large POW camp where men were starving and freezing to death.

Although our Viennese cook was efficient, our own diet had become monotonous; it consisted of a thick stew of potatoes, barley, or Russian millet, containing bits of meat. Together with a slice of the grey German army bread, the nourishment satisfied us; we were not required to do much physical work except for the bi-weekly drill. It was common knowledge that in case of food shortage or an unexpected increase in men, the kitchen staff would rectify the deficiency with a bucket of water or two. "As long as we have enough water, we will have soup." Often the supply roads became impassable during the winter, and we soon learned of the tasty large flat mushrooms that were in good supply in the surrounding needle forest and would complement our diet accordingly.

One day in the fall, one of our men was missing for his shift. On searching the surrounding area we found him close by, lying prone on the forest floor; he was shot dead while picking mushrooms. Foul play by marauding partisans was possible, and the cause of death was investigated. It turned out that the missile had entered his left lower lumbar area and exited in the right axilla. He had been struck accidentally by a stray shot fired from far away, perhaps to shoot a bird. Bending down toward a mushroom, he was in the path of the trajectory of the bullet returning to earth. Lt. Holtmann approached me about another letter to the victim's folks. To learn that their loved one had died as a consequence of a freak accident would not satisfy them. None of us had combat experience; we felt like tourists on an expedition. The fatal stray bullet that had killed was the only one our comrade ever encountered. Lt. Holtmann accepted my letter, kept in a heroic tone, including the expressions valiant, death on the field of honour, etc.

Although frivolous use of the strategic communication line was strictly *verboten,* I had no qualms using the military line from inside Russia to telephone my mother in Oldenburg. In fact, Mother installed a telephone at home for just that purpose. Once a week, I would check for a free TF channel, press the call button, and a courteous female voice would announce that I had reached "*Wolf's Schanze* switchboard," the Führer's headquarters. The operator was unaware that the call was from a lowly soldier instead of some high-brass general. I requested her to dial my mother's phone number in western Germany, long distance, and, presto, there was

Mom answering, free of charge, for as long as we wanted. The year was 1941, decades before the electronic age. I felt some satisfaction in abusing the system that we despised; for all I cared, our "glorious Führer" might die in his bunker without ever knowing about my transgression.

The winter nights in January were severe; our sleeping quarters, previous student dormitories, were unheated. The large TF room, crammed with electronic equipment, with hundreds of vacuum tubes glowing, was cozy warm, a desirable place for the off-duty crew. We were huddled closely together and had little opportunity to wash our bodies. Although there was no incidence of louse infestation, we received, quite unexpectedly, together with our reduced rations, huge amounts of sachets marked "Dr. Morell's Lice Powder" that we, despite its highly unpleasant odour, used quite liberally as an alternative to personal hygiene. The stench of the yellowish powders of potassium xanthogenate was nauseating. Post-war research reports indicate that the evil-smelling obscure concoction possesses absolutely no insecticidal property: *"We conducted an experiment with Rusla, Dr. Morell's Lice Powder, stored in a little box with lice. After twenty-four hours the lice crawled out in rollicking spirits."* Dr. Morell, personal physician to the Führer, had supreme sanction to put several factories to work to supply the German forces with his ineffective product.

During the dull hours of our shift in Pskow, while attending to the TF equipment, with nothing else to do but watch the vacuum tubes glow, the hours became boring. It was against regulations to enter or utilize the active telephone lines, except for technical reasons. We, however, used to scan the twenty-eight channels as we nowadays would change television channels or twiddle the radio dial to find the right program. This trespass into military secrets was strictly forbidden but impossible to enforce. Did we not have the duty to maintain and check the system constantly? To us, wire-tapping these strategic lines was an entertainment, both interesting and useful to obtain the latest information from the front. Added excitement came with advance orders to keep a certain channel clear and in good working condition. The notice was an indication that a *Blitz Gesprach*, a top level strategic conversation, was about to take place. On one of these occasions we "dropped in" on a discussion between Hitler and the commander of our Army Group North, Field Marshall Wilhelm von Leeb, tasked with the conquest of Leningrad. All available telephones and listening devices were used by those on and off duty. Although the eaves-dropping would weaken the signal, we just turned up the degree of amplification to restore a normal sound level. We heard every word that was said. By chance, our curiosity paid off; we had tapped into a TF channel that carried a historic conversation and shed light upon our own immediate future.

On regular shift at the Pskow TF station.

Ears glued to the phones at our station in Pskow, we
hear Hitler firing one of his best generals.

A moderate Glühwein Christmas party far away from home. Lieutenant Holtmann appears to condone young Lüdke's bold eccentricity of putting on his officer's cap.

During the effort to capture Leningrad, von Leeb had ordered a recent tactical retreat from the town of Tikhvin, a vital railhead, and the Russians had recaptured the place. Over the telephone line we were tapping into, we heard Hitler express his extreme annoyance. *Der Führer* saw retreat as a sign of German weakness. He reprimanded the general: "Where the German soldier stands, he stays put." He was quarrelling, castigating his officer. Field Marshall von Leeb, successful strategist and veteran of the German Army Staff throughout several campaigns, pointed out that, since the summer had come to an end and his troops were ill-prepared for a winter campaign, and since they still had not reached Leningrad, it might be prudent to put off the advance in the north and direct all forces against Moscow instead. He pleaded for "elastic resistance," yielding to Russian attacks, then advancing again on favourable situations, but temporizing the Leningrad winter operation by hibernating, sparing lives and weapons. We heard von Leeb even offer to deplete his own Army Group North of his renowned panzer divisions and transfer them to Army Group Centre for a decisive thrust against Moscow--the capital and centre of rail, road, and river navigation, and of the Russian war industry. He argued that at least twenty-five percent of armaments were produced in the city. Once Moscow was in German hands, the rest of Russia would collapse.

Von Leeb's arguments fell on the ears of an unsophisticated ex-corporal who was now supreme commander of he German *Wehrmacht*, whose "divine intuition" saw von Leeb's ideas as bordering on treason, who feared that once a retreat began it would become a setback. The few local withdrawals that Hitler himself had clumsily initiated led to such heavy losses of equipment that he became convinced that the only solution was an absolutely rigid defence. And that was how the winter campaign was going to be conducted. The arguments grew decisive with Hitler's final shout: "General, I expect you here in my headquarters tomorrow," and a hard slamming-down sound on the line followed by a much softer click. The phone went dead. The day was December 18, 1941. With our own ears we had witnessed Hitler firing one of his best. The terse altercation reminded me of the old carpet-seller joke. "*Mein Führer*, do you wish me to wrap the rug, or are you going to munch it right here?"

Viewing Field Marshall General von Leeb as a victim of the "carpet-biter" may have coloured my opinion. I had considered, although with reservations, the general as a fatherly figure, concerned about and caring for us who were his men, who had to give our lives for Germany. I had expected that von Leeb, as a Catholic, would be moderate and opposed to Hitler. After the war, from Canada, I uncovered devastating information. There are photographs of the "good" field marshall, as he personally, with his own hands, places the hanging noose on the necks of a young couple accused of being anti-German partisans. Although his nation has honoured him with posthumous homage--his grave protected with a shrine-like chapel on the Solin Cemetery in Bavaria, a new German military barracks named after him--the leader I once respected no longer deserves my veneration; in my eyes, Field Marshall von Leeb was a murderer.

Since the human slaughters in the German and Polish concentration camps at Buchenwald and Auschwitz, the world has witnessed other mass killings in South East Asia, the Russian Gulags, Milosevich's Bosnia and Herzegovina, Rwanda, and Iraq. Although too similar to Kosovo, the name of another killing place, Kovno, has not left my mind since I began writing down these memories. My search on von Leeb yielded an unexpected perk--a photograph in which I recognized the face of another killer, the butcher of Kovno, taking a break, leaning on the iron pipe he used, surrounded by his dead victims and some spectators. The caption identifies the perpetrator as Algirdas Antanas Pavalkis, standing in front of the Lietukis garage and gasoline station in Kovno. In the background above his left shoulder, it is possible to discern the faces of Erich Peters and myself, wearing soldiers' caps. How would I ever forget coming across that person and that place? While looking for bread, simple sustenance of life, I found death doled out in its most cruel form.

The butcher of Kovno.

Gerd Asche

Pavalkis reportedly stated that anger about Russian treatment of his family had inspired his actions. Further research uncovered an excerpt from the Nuremberg Trial Documents, a report on "spontaneous self-cleansing in Kovno," which confirms the clandestine role played by German Security Police in instigating the liberated population of Lithuania to "eliminate those left behind after the retreat of the Red Army."

Our TF eavesdropping had made us witness to Hitler's uncontrolled reaction which lead to the historic decision to sack von Leeb for his allegedly traitorous ideas. However, by the spring of 1942, the rejected plan seemed to have found some vindication. It was abandoned again because of the prospect of new military grandeur elsewhere. Closing a gigantic kettle around several Russian divisions near Kiev took priority over von Leeb's Moscow plan, and the last opportunity to win the war had slipped through Hitler's fingers. Monitoring the TF channels also indicated that our days in the Russian north were numbered. TF units were designed for a fast-moving forward advance over long distance. Hitler's decision had turned the Leningrad front into one of rigid static defence. Indeed, our services became redundant and we prepared for a change to another theatre of the war. TF1 Company's departure from Pskow would become symbolic of the future of *Armee Gruppe Nord* and prognostic for the outcome of the war.

Chapter 8

Our clandestine wiretapping had paid off; we were aware of an impending re-deployment even before our own superior officers knew about it. In the Führer's own words, our days in the Leningrad theatre of war were numbered. The questions remained: what was the strategic plan and where would we be going? Would it be to France? Would we return to Germany to get ready for the invasion of Britain, or would we be engaged somewhere on the Russian front? Absurdly, we would find the answer in the width of the railroad tracks, in the difference between the wider gauge of the Russian railroad and the narrower one of the western European countries. Goods from Russian freight trains required labourious reloading at the border. To save tactical time, troops and material destined for the west would motor by road as far as the Russian border to be loaded directly onto European standard gauge railroad cars. What would the future hold for us? Would it be road or rail? The answer came: to proceed to the Pskow rail yard and load our vehicles on Russian flatbeds, ruling out a western European destination; we would remain on the eastern front in support of another planned blitz advance.

Our train headed southeast and kept rolling for days; stops were usually in the middle of nowhere within an ocean of sunflowers. We would line up on the tracks with our mess gear at the kitchen car for a hot meal or rations, and resume our journey through the sunny Ukraine. After passing Kiev, we unloaded at Stalino on the river Donets, an industrial town of rows of workers' apartment buildings with water toilets that did not flush for lack of water. We had to dig latrines and made friends with the enthused local people. Our journey continued as a motorized column to Rostov on the Don River. Following the German advance, code-named Operation Edelweiss (the name of an alpine flower), we turned southeast to the oil-rich Caucasus region.

After the winter campaign in the north, our TF Company was assigned to the southern front. During a day of rest near Stalino, we used the time to improve our language skills by cavorting with two Ukrainian beauties.

One of Hitler's grandiose plans involved eliminating the Russian Black Sea fleet and using tankers to bring Russian oil into central Europe via the Danube River. Would he perhaps follow in the footsteps of the Bavarian king and re-activate the old Ludwig's Kanal, a remnant of the failed attempt to connect the Danube River with the Rhine? To prevent interference with the push for the oil and the refineries of Baku, the Germans created, on purpose, a point of conflict hundreds of miles to the north as a battleground that would keep the Russians busy. They chose Stalingrad for this diversion. Little did the German general staff realize that the Stalingrad venture would cost them dearly. The strategists had reached their turning point in the same way the Romans met their fate in 216 BC near the town of Cannae, when Hannibal defeated the Roman legions under Varro and Aemilio in a great slaughter. As Moscow was to Napoleon, when success turned to failure, so would Stalingrad become the Cannae for Hitler and his General Paulus.

Stalingrad was a turning point for Nazi Germany reminiscent of the way the Russian winter had forced Napoleon to retreat in 1812.

For the time being, however, our speed of advance was unrestricted and seemed a repetition of the Barbarossa summer campaign in the north. Without resistance, in tourist-style, we reached Mineralnye Wody, known for its mineral water, and Pyatigorsk, once an elegant spa town for the ruling classes where nineteenth century czars used to have their vacation homes. The climate was pleasant; peaches, grapes, and figs grew in abundance. The white cone of Mount Elbrus dominated the landscape. We were housed in solid stone houses; the town square was adorned with classical colonnaded buildings reminding me of pictures I had seen of St. Marcus Square in Venice. As German soldiers, we mingled freely with the friendly Georgians in the town and frequented their shops for a piece of cake and a cup of honey-sweetened Russian tea. One sunny afternoon, while the streets were filled with promenading Saturday shoppers, we heard a solitary Russian plane circling the city at low altitude. A huge explosion shattered the peaceful atmosphere. I ran outside and saw on the wide city square a mass of corpses, severed arms and legs and other body parts; people were moaning. Dropping bombs on a civilian hinterland population had no tactical value except to upset the local people who were of a different ethnicity. It was a sobering reminder that we were in hostile territory, and we became more reserved in fraternizing with the locals.

As if the bombing had been a signal, the fortunes of war turned against us in the battle of Stalingrad, threatening encirclement of our entire *Armee Gruppe Süd* in the Caucasus. Since TF1 Company was most valuable to the war effort, we were one of the first units to be evacuated. Taking along all our equipment, we got out by the skin of our teeth. Because of lack of fuel, a paradoxical situation in the oil-rich region, a freight train took us through the bottleneck at Rostov. I did not realize how close we were to being taken prisoners until I heard the rumbling of cannon through the open door of our rolling freight car as we exited enemy territory.

Our train was adaptable to different track gauges, and we continued the journey by rail through Poland and Germany directly to the French town of Besançon on the river Doubs where we were to receive refresher training and additional drill. In this ancient place, we enjoyed bathing in the river weirs, having the water run over us. Our quarters consisted of a school complex; schools and education were usually the first to give way to war. The peaches were as sweet in Besançon as those grown in the Caucasus. I bought a whole flat, and we ate them all.

That night, a shot rang out in the room next to ours. One of my comrades had shot himself in the head. He was the soldier who, during our advance on Leningrad, had boasted of his escapades with the wife, and the following night, with the daughter, of a Lithuanian pastor whom the retreating Russians had abducted. The Baltic people had been happy to demonstrate their friendship with the German liberators. This young whippersnapper had abused their pro-German hospitality. However, that had been a year earlier. Why did he have to kill himself now? Was it his conscience that made him take the step? He may have been homesick. I'm certain it was not the peaches I had bought.

There was no funeral service; the body was sent home to Germany, and it was Holtmann's duty to contact the boy's mother. There was no question about who would draft the dismal letter. I was excused from drill practice to put the sepulchral words to paper. This time, I omitted ethical expressions; there would be no "fatherland" or "dying on the field of honour." Instead, I placed the onus strictly on the Third Reich and Adolf Hitler whom I despised, whose shoulders carried the responsibility for the deaths of millions. This bold action would, I hoped, end my letter-writing career. Holtmann, I anticipated, would tear the letter up in disgust. Unexpectedly, he accepted my concoction of political Nazi catchwords without comment. I felt sorry for the dead boy's mother who would have to drown her sorrows in a conglomeration of meaningless political phrases.

A large part of France was under German rule, and we were settling into the routine of an occupation force with military drill and free time for visiting the town, eating out in French restaurants, and getting French-style haircuts. There were German shows and regular mail from home. The town had many brothels; I witnessed a public demonstration in a beer hall. With the door wide open to the street and crowds of soldiers milling about, they were doing a roaring business in beer and wine. A prostitute was squatting over a German soldier who was lying on a table. Following his ejaculation, the boy got down, his face red from exertion and embarrassment. We watched another woman demonstrate her skill in picking up a ten-franc piece from the table edge without using her hands. She straddled the edge and picked up the coin with her vagina. I think she used the adductor muscles of her thighs since the outer vagina is void of constricting functions. No one was interested; besides, ten francs was quite a bit of money.

We received a lot of physical drill and expected to be allocated to some theatre of military action at any time. Besançon was our holding area; we enjoyed the beautiful weather and our life was getting comfortable until the quiet was disrupted by the news that the Allies had landed in Sicily on July 10, 1943. A new military front had opened up, dictating a German military reaction to back our Italian ally. Our TF1 Company was going to move south. Without delay, we motored to Austria and stayed in a school at Bad Ischl, close to the Italian border, anxiously awaiting the order to advance via the Brenner Pass into the country that the German poet Goethe cherished in his book "Italian Journey,

> Do you know the land where the lemon trees blossom?
> Among dark leaves the golden oranges glow.
> A gentle breeze from blue skies drifts.
> The myrtle is still, and the laurel stands high.
> Do you know it well?
> There, there would I go with you, my beloved.

The strategic Brenner Pass, once the border between Austria and Italy, became a gate where visitors from Italy entered the newly-created Greater German Reich.

Chapter 9

TF1 company had arrived in Bolzano, the first Italian town south of the Brenner Pass, and as our vehicles pulled up in the market square, we realized that none of us could speak a word of Italian. However, I soon found a solution in the language's striking similarity to classical Gymnasium-learned Latin; the much-flouted "dead" language was an amazing working substitute. I was, unexpectedly, assigned as an unofficial interpreter to a small advance column of five vehicles under Lieutenant Holtmann. We moved south along the Etsch, the Adige River, and the east coast of scenic Lake Garda until we reached the front of the local school in the town of Garda on the lake's south shore. For accommodation, the school building was requisitioned; in mild weather, we pitched our tents on the lawn of the school playground.

A brief break at Torbole, near the north end of the scenic Lake Garda in northern Italy.

Next to the schoolyard was a branch of the *Banca Popolare di Verona* as well as the residence of the bank manager who bore the unforgettable operatic name of Othello, reminding me of Verdi's opera by that name. The Othellos were friendly people who offered us, their newly-arrived allies, hot soup called minestrone. Mr. Othello's attractive young sister-in-law Lina Scapini was visiting from Verona, and during the next few days Lina and I enjoyed some pleasant hours together. The weather was balmy; we swam in the lake and exposed our bodies to the sunshine. The intimate contact advanced the level of my conversational Italian immeasurably. The Scapinis invited me to Verona and, in Italian hospitality, treated me generously to polenta, salami, and other local delights, including the local Bardolino wine. I became aware, however, that the family's interest in me extended beyond international north-south-axis friendship, and when Lina started taking German lessons in Verona, the town that after all was the setting of Shakespeare's great love play *Romeo and Juliet*, the order to move TF1 Company south came none too soon. It was probably a good thing for both of us.

For a long time I lost contact with Lina. Twenty years later, after the war, I visited Italy again and was able to track her down. She had married, and the couple had spent ten years in Venezuela where they did well. With the money earned, they had bought a motel on the east side of Lake Garda. Although their business lagged behind the five-star tourism of Fasano and Gardone on the west shore, I could tell that Lina had lived the good life; she had metamorphosed into a matronly and sedate *Signora*, deflating my expectations of enjoying the lively crisp beauty of earlier days. "For you and I are past our dancing days." (*Romeo and Juliet*)

Our TF1 Company moved a few hundred kilometres south, to a rural town called Sermide in the broad valley of the Po River, and again the local school became our quarters. My role as an unofficial company interpreter, clarifying disputes and settling business, came with the perk of some unusual tasks and liberties. A messenger from Dottore Pellegrini, the local physician, requested a conference about an important matter and I went to see him, expecting that he might ask for some help in the interest of his community. The visit was brief and sobering. I was shocked when I learned of his problem: he complained that he was short of coffee and wanted me to sell him twenty pounds! The doctor's request reflected the public's general esteem of their military--corruption was assumed to be the norm. Our own morning "coffee" was an ersatz concoction of ground-up roasted barley; I myself had not drunk real coffee for years. Besides, I was an interpreter and not in the business of selling military property.

A more enjoyable encounter was my meeting Miss Maria Freddi, a nineteen-year-old student who attended college in Ferrara. Maria was not only attractive; she was witty, intelligent, full of charm, and seemed to have taken a liking to me. Our connection was unaffected by political or military actions and remained cordial despite a significant change in the relationship between Germany and Italy that took place during my amorous pursuit in Sermide.

Maria Freddi from Sermide, a college student in Ferrara.

Italy had been under the dictatorship of Benito Mussolini who came to power with the support of his Black Shirts, brigades of unemployed Italian war veterans, around 1923. Ten years later, Hitler closely followed the Duce's example, relying on the Brown Shirts, the *Sturm Abteilung* (SA), who would spread fear and terror in pogroms and initiate "spontaneous" demonstrations as they did in the disgraceful *Kristallnacht* of 1938. The two like-minded dictators, both ex-corporals, had met for the first time in Vienna in June of 1934, and their two countries proclaimed to constitute the north-south axis of Europe.

It was during the time of my romance with Maria, in the summer of 1943, when we learned of a *coup d'etat* that led to Mussolini's arrest by Romans who were tired of fascism and war. The Duce had been spirited away to an unknown location where he was held in protective custody. King Victor Emmanuel III, the new Head of State, appointed Marshall Pietro Badoglio as his supreme commander. Badoglio promptly signed an armistice agreement with General Dwight Eisenhower on behalf of all of Italy, although the greater part of the peninsula was still occupied by the German *Wehrmacht*, still allied officially with Italy's deposed Duce. To the German General Kesselring, in control of the Italian boot north of Rome, Badoglio's surrender was treason, a hostile act against Germany, Italy's previous friend and brother-in-arms. The unexpected surrender had turned us into an occupation force. Then, making matters worse, the Italy in the south declared war against the Italy of the north, and the ensuing hostilities would invoke German military domination. There were now two Italian governments, one on each side, and the struggle took on the character of a civil war.

To us in northern Italy, the change in relationship did not become obvious right away with the exception of one significant military proclamation: every Italian possessing a firearm had to surrender the weapon immediately. The response in Sermide was prompt, and a large pile, mostly of handguns, accumulated on the tables in a classroom of the school where we were quartered. Some of my comrades were interested in the firearms and had free access to the pile of handguns, an unusual opportunity to handle the weapons. Suddenly, a shot rang out; a soldier collapsed. The Berretta pistol he held had discharged into his thigh; the bullet severed the femoral artery. Only immediate deep vascular surgery or amputation would have kept him from bleeding to death. None of us had medical or first-aid knowledge, and the local caffeine addict, Dottore Pellegrini, was no help. The soldier bled to death amongst the tables loaded with revolvers and pistols.

The previous three losses of life loomed to my mind: one man run over by a tank backing up, a mushroom picker killed in Pskow by a stray bullet, and the suicide in Besancon. They were useless deaths and could have been avoided. It again seemed my task to write to a widow about her husband's futile death on the field of honour, for Führer and Fatherland. I acted in conviction and good faith to modify the incident of fooling around with an unfamiliar pistol in the classroom of a country school in northern Italy. From the meagre source of my twenty-three years' life experience, my condolence spoke less of the grand finale of a hero's final summons and were more to the fact, expressing the lieutenant's (and my) true feelings that we, his comrades, had enjoyed his friendship and good-natured company, and the TF Company would miss him.

With the Duce out of the picture, events in Italy developed rapidly. Sermide was designated as the jumping-off point for our next move in a war of the north against the south, principally a war between Germany and the American allies on Italian soil. TF1 Company moved south, as far as the Trasimene Lake, a place whose name I remember vaguely as the scene of an historic battle between Hannibal and the Romans under their impetuous consul Flaminius in 217 BC. Two thousand years later, our unit would be located not far from the scene of Hannibal's victory of antiquity. Since the German front was moved back, we shifted to the safety of the wine-growing region of Tuscany. On our way, our commander allowed a few hours to drive into the city of Florence, the cradle of Renaissance. However, most buildings were sandbagged against war damage; Michelangelo's marble statue of David had been removed from the front of the Palazzo Vecchio to a safer place. It was small compensation for our group of four to have our picture taken with the Arno River and the city in the background as a memento of the occasion.

High above the bank of the Arno River, overlooking the city of Florence.

We set up our TF booster station on a farm south of Florence near Siena, an old university town, surrounded by hilly vineyards. The owner of the farm must have been evicted or jailed for some political reason, likely a loyalist; we never heard from him. Rosa, a nineteen-year-old girl, became our cook and housekeeper. For the rest, we were on our own, serving as an important communication link between Kesselring's front and the Führer's headquarters. Our main meal of the day, mostly homemade pasta, was enhanced considerably through the keenness of one of my men, Heinz Schreiber, who regularly furnished our dinner table with a decanter of full-bodied red wine. It must have been a good vintage; a glassful with our meal brought on the need for a postprandial nap. Heinz had gone over the house and discovered three large barrels in the basement, presumably containing wine. Although our activity was restricted to the use of the house as a technical accommodation, Heinz had used a fine pocket auger to drill one cask, releasing a thin stream of pure *Chianti Colli Senesi*. He closed the hole with a matchstick for further daily use. Although the amount removed was insignificant, I realized that we were committing an act of theft.

It may have been the contact with Lina, the Scapini family in Verona, and my intimate conversations with Maria Freddi in Sermide, augmented by my knowledge of classical Latin, that enhanced my linguistic abilities and made me acceptable to one of Siena's more prominent families. Or, I may simply have been the last resort in a desperate search for help. A Bugatti car with Italian license plates drove up the narrow lane one day. We received a visit from a prominent Sienese gentleman, Dottore Lenzi, an internal medicine specialist and head of the medical department of Siena University, and his wife Leonora. They had not come on an altruistic medical or social mission, however. Their request was for personal help, and they took me into their confidence. The family was in distress, concerned about the fate of the doctor's brother Capitano Lorenzo Lenzi, commander of a *sommergibile*, a submarine, that had been in action during the American landing at Anzio and was overdue for its return to the naval base. The family had received no news from Lorenzo. With the changes of government in Rome and the official state of war existing between the two Italys, compounded by the German occupation and the American invasion, long distance telephone connections were blocked. The Lenzis feared that the submarine commander might have perished with his boat. Could I help them to resolve their dilemma?

I took them to the technical room, activated one of the twenty-eight channels, pressed the call button, and asked the switchboard operator for the naval base in La Spezia. Instead of the expected reply in German language from the naval base in La Spezia, I received a response in Italian from a military telephone exchange in now American-occupied Rome, and quickly handed the receiver to Dr. Lenzi. He was able to have the switchboard operator in the south, in Rome, in the now hostile part of Italy, connect him with La Spezia in the northern German-occupied part of the country, locating his brother and finally talking to him directly. Doctor Lenzi and his wife were relieved.The submarine commander could officially have been deemed an enemy since Badoglio's armistice and his declaration of war against northern Italy and Germany, but telephone connections had not kept pace with political and military developments. The relationships seemed confusing; we had used the German military TF communications network to penetrate the now hostile Italian system as far as Rome and, without effort, were re-routed to the German-controlled Italian north, an unheard of lack of military security that raised the question whether the reverse process, entering the German system, was equally easy to bring off. Were it not for my restricted knowledge of English, I might have been able to talk my way to General Eisenhower's desk! We rejoiced in our successful contribution to local peoples' peace of mind. The Lenzis were greatly relieved and obligated and invited me to some of their fine Italian dinners where they introduced me to Dr. Lenzi's father-in-law, Professor Izar, the dean of medicine at Siena University. In this peaceful atmosphere, our social life and the independent *dolce vita* were left undisturbed as long as we would maintain adequate function of the booster station for *Der Führer's* telephone connection to General Kesselring's headquarters.

One day in May of 1944, I received a call from my company commander, Lt. Holtmann. It was shortly after the allied advance past Monte Casino; the tactical need for a German retreat to the north was pending. "Asche, we have designated your location near Siena as a midway place for a fuel depot in case TF1 has to retreat. Find a suitable bomb-proof storage space for "Benzine" (gasoline) for our vehicles to tank up on the way north!"

The order was reminiscent of his request of three years previous when I was ordered to find bread in the Lithuanian city of Kovno, except that this time I would be able to oblige without difficulty. I knew of two large open but well-concealed caves on the hillside above us, a fine viewpoint, overlooking the town of Siena a few miles away. The caves could be closed in. I received orders to have the reservoir constructed. Truckloads of requisitioned bricks arrived from a nearby plant, and bricklayers secured the opening with a three-foot-deep wall and a metal door.

While supervising the construction, I had paid little attention to a local fellow stringing nets in the bushes nearby. His activity was unusual, and I became aware that he was a bird catcher, reminding me of the legendary Papageno, the bird catcher in Mozart's *Magic Flute* fantasy. When I saw his helper, a blonde girl, I thought of Papagena, Papageno's fabulous assistant, and some of Mozart's tunes came to my mind. One late afternoon, as I hiked uphill to inspect the progress of the day's construction work, the usually bucolic quiet was disturbed by the noise of heavy traffic drifting up from the valley below. On the main road leading past Siena, a long motorized military column of tanks, heavy trucks, artillery, personnel carriers and other vehicles was travelling south, stretching for a mile or more, obviously moving to back up the Italian resistance against the British-American advance. To my surprise, Papagena appeared. I invited her to sit on the grass beside me for the unusual bird's eye show below. The girl was attractive and exuded sexuality, and soon our rising personal amativeness made us ignore the noisy spectacle below. The traffic sounds became an insignificant background drone, and we reclined in the high grass. She had begun kissing with her mouth open when, like a divine reprimand, bolts of thunder and lightning from heaven, a volley of explosions from directly above, stunned us out of our Freudian reverie. Engorgements wilted; we threw ourselves into the grassy furrow, no longer to deepen our intimacy, but for plain survival. I thought this was retribution, and that the end had come.

Gerd Asche

The cause of the disturbance were two American fighter planes that had appeared out of nowhere and were strafing the German column below. Because of our elevation, they were just a few metres above us when they began firing. There was pandemonium on the road, with smoke and fire. Vehicles exploded, and the entire column came to a halt. We were shocked and very much afraid. That was the only time in Italy during the war when I experienced enemy action at such close range and on such an untimely occasion. The attack must have severely frightened the girl; no bird, neither one in the net nor a swarm in the bush, would bring back Papagena or Papageno.

We were startled to see American fighter planes attack our troops so far from the front, until Dr. Lenzi came up with the answer. An American aircraft carrier with thirty fighter planes had anchored near Livorno, a few miles off the Liguria coast. The allied noose was tightening. Although the action had not been directed at us, we anticipated more patrols and assaults from the carrier's planes. The pilots might spot the piles of fresh red leftover bricks on our construction site. I had to get rid of the conspicuous target immediately and arranged with the contractors to speed up the work and remove redundant building material to render the place as it was before. Bricks were a valuable commodity during a time of severe material shortage; to get the brightly visible material off the hill, I offered to sell them at a bargain price on the first day but threatened to raise the price every day thereafter. In the end, the project was completed without enemy interference; the depot served its purpose; the fuel helped our company vehicles to escape north. However, the Allied progress was inexorable until it stopped at the "Gothic Line," the German line of defense near Bologna. Saving Rome, the cradle of classical civilization, from destruction, the German high command had voluntarily declared the town an open city and evacuated all German offices, including the embassy.

Meanwhile, German intelligence had made an important discovery. They had located the hiding place of the captured Mussolini, a small inaccessible hotel, a ski resort on Mount Gran Sasso in the Abruzzi Mountains. Hitler commissioned the SS Captain Skorzeny to free his long-time friend and ally. In a daring raid, using motor-less sailplanes to land silently, and the renowned *Fieseler Storch* short-field-take-off airplane to fly him out, Mussolini was liberated. Reinstated over the part of Italy under German occupation, he reluctantly resumed the *pro forma* leadership. It soon became apparent, however, who the new master was. The Germans designated the only place on Lake Garda fitting the denomination "town," a place called Salo, as the seat of the new government to accommodate the Duce and his puppet cabinet. Salo became the government seat of the "Republic of Salo" and its facade ministries for external affairs, culture, justice, and finance. The location was selected for its inaccessibility--a narrow shore road, hemmed in on one side by the lake and on the other by steep mountain cliffs. For several kilometres, the highway disappears from view and continues as tunneled sections. It was a judiciously chosen trap for potential infiltrators, a confine, degrading an unreliable ally into a prisoner, a hostage. An allied advance into northern Italy was unlikely in the near future.

A low-power radio station, "Radio Victoria," became the official voice of the new government. A new ambassador, Rudolf Rahn, was appointed as head of the German delegation. His predecessor had been fired because he had been unaware of the King's treason and the planned arrest of Mussolini. In fact, Ambassador Mackensen in his ignorance had sent a telegram to Berlin on the day of the Duce's removal, advising that his position was never stronger. The new German embassy was established in the elaborate Beach Hotel Fasano, near Mussolini's seat of government in Salo on the west shore of Lago di Garda. Hotel Fasano is now a refurbished five-star hotel.

At our location north of Siena, my personal and official adversities began to mount. There was the now-completed building project to worry about and the unexpected attack of the American fighter planes on the advancing German military column that had been nearly eliminated in front of our eyes while we were engaged making love. Despite the illegal hustle, I was glad to be rid of the remaining red bricks. The closeness of the aircraft carrier off the Ligurian coast was disturbing. However, once the highway below us was cleared of the burned-out remnants and the brick wall of the gasoline depot painted green, we offered no military target to attract the planes. Admittedly, using the German military communication system to call about Dr. Lenzi's brother and receiving the good news of his surviving the U-boat adventure at Anzio was a transgression but, in my eyes, it was a good deed to the local community without strategic consequences. We learned of the German General Kesselring's withdrawal from Rome, leaving it an open city and precluding German armed resistance or war damage to historical sites. Mussolini's abduction, the Italian Marshall Badoglio's armistice with the allies, his subsequent declaration of war against his own people, topped by the Allies' landing south of Rome at Anzio, their conquest of Monte Cassino, the move of the German embassy out of Rome, while the invasion of Normandy was ongoing in northern France--to me, it was progress, each episode a step closer to the end of the war. Then there was news of the discovery of the missing Italian dictator and his spectacular rescue and reinstatement. All these confusing uncertain conditions culminated in a telephone call from Lt. Holtmann. What outlandish request, what exotic order was my commander going to issue this time? Unexpectedly, he tersely advised me that he was recalling me from Siena.

Where had I gone wrong? I thought I had done a good job, admittedly not out of patriotism or the desire to win the war, but merely as a personal challenge to complete a non-combative project. I was disappointed to be taken off the site but soon learned that there was nothing punitive about my reassignment. The order was to return north, to Lake Garda, the new place of movers and shakers, to set up a TF terminal for the German embassy in Fasano, linking it with communications to Hitler in Berlin and General Kesselring who still seemed to hold the German front north of Rome.

The Roman god Janus behind us on the wall would turn if he could, upset at the military violating the diplomatic sanctum of the German embassy.

The three-man crew at the embassy TF station takes to the fresh air.

When Klaus Voigt (with glasses) arranged for a photograph of the two of us as Christmas greetings for home, NCO Baumgartner insisted that he be included.

My quarters at the embassy, a private room in the Villa Maria, adjoined the embassy, and although in military uniform, we had direct access to the embassy's inner civilian courtyard, flouting the usually observed distinction between diplomats and military personnel. The climate and working conditions were pleasant; the members of the embassy treated us as part of their civilian office staff. My comrade Klaus Voigt had arranged to have our picture taken by the embassy photographer; we would send the cards home as a unique Christmas greeting. Sergeant Baumgartner, visiting from Company Headquarters, insisted, nay, ordered us, to have him included, and as a result of his imposition, the picture was taken with Baumgartner seated in the centre. Perhaps his loneliness made him abuse his authority, spoiling my plan for a personal Christmas greeting to Mother.

Although we were only simple soldiers, the embassy had invited us to attend their Christmas party. The buffet offered an unheard-of cornucopia of delights--tropical fruit, real oranges and bananas, pineapples, grapes, and peaches. Smoked pheasant, oysters, cheeses, and salamis shared the buffet with cork-popping Champagnes, Asti Spumante, the local smooth, full-bodied red Bardolino , or the rich and fruity Valpolicella wine, and as much of it as we could drink. As simple "krauts," however, we stayed much in the background, somewhat awed by the assembly of ladies in peacetime cocktail dresses and coat-tailed bow-tied gentlemen diplomats.

An attractive young lady approached me and introduced herself as Gisela Quitzau. A few glasses of Bardolino turned our affinity to mutual affection, and Gisela told me confidentially that she was associated with the German naval attaché whose office was located in nearby Merano in South Tyrol. Since there was no German marine activity to speak of, with only two damaged U-boats moored in the naval shipyards at La Spezia, she was on temporary "loan" to the embassy in Fasano. We discussed literature; I asked for her favourite author. She turned out to be an eccentric, reading the Chinese poet Li Tai Po, who had written "The Song of the Earth," a poem that became the Austrian composer Gustav Mahler's theme to write a symphony, a tone poem, under the same title. Here I had found a person who shared my interests; we spent the rest of the evening together and parted with a plan for the next day, a weekend. Gisela knew of a park in nearby Gardone where a ship's bow formed the memorial over the grave of the Italian war hero and poet Gabriele D'Annuncio. Our hours together became days together, away from the cruel and brutal realities of the war, and we smoked a good number of *cigarettes après*. We would meet at my small apartment where I had discovered an inconspicuous access door from the beach, an unknown Achilles' heel to the embassy's security, that allowed Gisela to bypass the heavily-guarded main entrance and avoid inquisitive looks from the sentries. Our pleasant association in Fasano grew but ended abruptly when work called her back to her own desk.

Assistant Naval Attache Gisela Quitzau holidayed at Lake Garda where we met at the embassy Christmas party.

As a member of the diplomatic staff, Gisela would have had the means to keep in contact, I have never again heard from her. What was a memorable landmark, a milestone, in my life, may have been a short, ephemeral interlude in her colourful diplomatic career. Recalling the events many years later prompted me to turn to the Internet to investigate Gisela's fate after the war. A Gisela Quitzau is listed in the Long Island Journal of the New York Times of July 1988, visiting an art gallery with her Jewish friend Rudi Loeb who later changed into Rudi Lawrence. I discovered her birth year as 1916, and that she died in 2001, aged eighty-five. Thinking of my relationship, the street graffito comes to mind:

> *Vivere per amare* (live to love)
> *amare per soffrire* (love to suffer)
> *soffrire per morire* (suffer to die)

Although Gisela's departure from Fasano had brought our love to a sudden standstill, my private relationships in Italy were not at an end, however. Initiated by my desire to meet people and make friends, promoted further by the increasing quality of my conversational Italian, which none of my comrades was attempting to acquire, these episodes of personal friendship were brief and restricted to the duration of my unit's stay at a particular placement and ceased abruptly in keeping with our company's change of location. Such was the case in my involvement with Maria Freddi. As Gisela had left unexpectedly without a trace, so had I been compelled to leave Maria Freddi behind in Sermide when Mussolini's arrest demanded our immediate departure, moving south. My sudden disappearance must have been painful for the clean, innocent girl. She was special and of good character and determined to maintain our emotional ties.

Although receiving written correspondence was non-existent except for occasional letters from Mother, one day the embassy's postal clerk handed me a postcard that had been mailed from within Italy and arrived in their diplomatic pouch, forwarded by the *Poste Italiane*. Instead of a Mussolini postage stamp, it bore the face of King Vittorio Emmanuel, the re-instated head of state in the south. However, as a sign of the re-emerged Mussolini government in the north, the King's image was marred by a red fascist symbol stamped across his face. The card's obverse depicted the castle of Ferrara, the postcard's point of mailing, and bore my name and rank in correct official military abbreviation as well as my address, Villa Maria in Fasano, on Lago di Garda. It must have taken the sender some effort to penetrate the German military system to determine not only my rank and the exact German acronym of my rank, but also to find my location. The postcard was from Maria Freddi who, in firm, mature handwriting, assured me of her love and everlasting affection, written, of course, in Italian. She must have had problems in obtaining the data and transferring the postcard via the Italian postal system into the German military *Feld Post* and the embassy's diplomatic mailbag. However, the Germans employed many local workers, and what warm-blooded Italian would not be overwhelmed by the well-written message of love and affection and expedite the amorous message pronto, even by resorting to diplomatic channels.

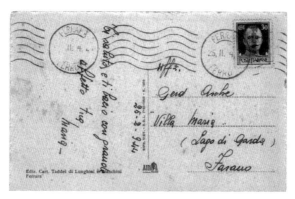

It was all about Amore!

There was one person among the embassy staff at Fasano whose appearance made me feel very uncomfortable. He was an officer in the black uniform of Hitler's notorious SS. His presence brought back to my mind the brutal slaughter in Kovno. I suspected him to be a political Gestapo officer, assigned to assure adherence to proper Nazi protocol by the embassy's staff. He requested to see me. I was apprehensive, fearing an impending indoctrination and a reprimand for my breach of security by using the hidden beach door. I felt insecure; could perhaps a slip of my tongue during the Christmas party have let out an improper remark reviling the Nazi party or the person of our Führer?

I need not have worried. His eyes were friendly behind the impressive rank of SS *Obersturmbannführer.* The feared black uniform covered the pleasant and sociable personality of Franz Spögler who explained that his fancy apparel was to demonstrate a status of high security and served to deter unwelcome visitors. Officer Spögler had come to discuss with me a matter of strategic concern. He explained that he was the officer responsible for the safety of Benito Mussolini who was suffering from depression and mental confusion. After the stress of his arrest in Rome and his incarceration on Mount Gran Sasso, he had been "liberated" against his will. The breakneck escape and Hitler's expectation of his resuming the role of governing the country had made the Duce despondent; he would rather have been left in peace at the ski hotel.

Franz Spögler came to the point: the Führer himself had approved the ambassador's plan to assign four of the embassy's twenty-eight TF channels to Mussolini's offices in Salo as an appeasement. Ostensibly an opportunity to communicate with the skeleton remnants of his Italian forces, to Mussolini, the link was in reality nothing more than a toy.

To prevent unpredictable action by the Duce, possibly a coup d'etat against the German Reich, Franz Spögler, in addition to serving as his bodyguard, was to monitor the Duce's activity and requested me to perform the technical work of "looping" the designated channels through the embassy's security system. He took me to the main building and unlocked a bedroom assigned to him. The room contained some of Spögler's things. The bed appeared not to have been slept in. The trouble was, he agonized, that the Duce's personality had changed since his capture; he was subject to capricious mood swings, and his activity required continuous attention. Franz unlocked a built-in closet and asked me to wire the four designated channels to a panel in the wardrobe to enable him to listen in on the Duce's conversations. He gave me the keys to both the room and the cabinet and left me to it. I could have told Franz that we were old hands at tapping into telephone lines and eavesdropping on the conversations of prominent leaders, including the Führer himself. However, he need not worry about our trustworthiness; unlike Franz who spoke Italian fluently, none of us would be able to understand the language well enough. We carried out the installation, including small lights indicating when a channel was in use, left some headphones, locked the cabinet and the room and returned the keys.

I began to like Franz. For a member of the SS, he deported himself more pleasantly and reasonably than expected and we actually became friends. He had been recruited for his German-Austrian origin and was disdainful of his Italian citizenship and of Rome's rule imposed on the people of South Tyrol, a region that had become Italian at Austria's expense as a result of the 1919 Treaty of Versailles. In general, Franz argued, Hitler had strongly denounced and flouted the so-called Versailles Peace Dictate, vastly exceeding the 100,000-man restriction of the German army and repossessing almost all of the territory previously taken away. Germany and Austria had reunited. Had not French Alsace-Lorraine become German Elsass-Lothringen again? Was not the previous Polish Corridor reunited with Germany as the Ost Mark, and had not the Sudeten Land, the German-settled part of Czechoslovakia, been the excuse to embrace the entire country into the Reich? The slogan for the Germans and Austrians abroad was "Home into the Reich!" Yet, Franz complained, his own country, South Tyrolia, remained unreclaimed by the Führer who would not move a finger for the return of the South Tyrolese to German-speaking Austria. This fellow Hitler, although an Austrian by birth himself, had deserted and sold the country of his brothers and sisters for the price of the tenuous friendship with this Italian gigolo and dictator. That uneven bargain was the reason for the resentment of Franz Spögler and other Tyrolese against the very person for whose safety he was now responsible, whom he must supervise, to whose every word he was required to listen even when the now-defunct dictator fancied to telephone his mistress.

I soon found out that Franz Spögler's SS appearance did not reflect his political conviction either. He had been put into the uniform out of convenience and to give the embassy set-up more authority. Who wants to tangle with the SS? Once we had revealed our common political standpoint, Franz took me in his Volkswagen on a visit to his family in the Dolomites, a place called Lengomoos, where he and his wife operated a farm and guesthouse. In fact, most of the farms and hotels there were owned and operated by Spöglers, all relatives, living fairly isolated and away from cities like Bolzano. Mrs. Spögler, a dark-haired Tyrolean woman served us a *Jausen*, in Austrian, a small meal with sandwiches of smoked beef, the meat sliced paper thin for better flavour. The visit took all day, and after our return to Fasano it seemed that we had gained each other's full trust and confidence. It was by a curious incident that I learned of my new friend's additional, more delicate assignment.

Franz brought me a small table radio that would not operate properly. This was the time before the invention of transistors; the set operated on vacuum glass tubes similar to our military TF panels which contained hundreds of them. The construction was unfamiliar; the German radios that I used to repair contained a transformer to generate the power to heat the tube filaments. This much lighter Italian apparatus traded convenience for safety; the valves or tubes were connected in series and directly exposed to the full power of the electrical outlet without an insulating transformer. I discovered that one electronic part, the cathode resistor, was partly burned out and thus affected the function of all the other tubes that were connected in-line, similar to one defective Christmas light bulb preventing the rest of the string from lighting up. After replacing the resistor, the little radio functioned again.

As Franz was away, the embassy desk asked me to deliver the set personally to its owner, a Miss Petacci, in the nearby Villa Fiordaliso. When I knocked at the door, I encountered security precautions; the Signorina expressed fear that people might try to kill her. She was thankful for my service, offered no compensation, but confided that she could again enjoy the Duce's broadcasts from "Radio Victoria." The identity of this attractive redhead dawned on me. It seemed that prominent men in Italy, unofficially but quite openly, keep a woman, a mistress, besides their spouse, and so did Mussolini keep Claretta Petacci. While his wife Donna Rachele and two children occupied a residence near Salo, about ten kilometres to the south, his mistress was living almost next door. On my way out, Miss Petacci introduced me to an elderly brittle gentleman, her father, who, she said, was the retired personal physician to Pope Pius XI, and I told the old gentleman of my plans to become a physician also. Now I understood Franz Spögler's duties; at night he spent his time as Claretta's guard and watchman while by day he kept his eye on her lover Benito.

When I returned to my comrades at our TF station, they asked me about this lady's attributes. I had to concede that while she was not unattractive, I saw in her a frightened, confused human being. Earlier, Franz had also expressed to me his concern for the safety of this lonesome woman and her horrible fate in case she should ever be captured. He had, he confided, designated a place of refuge for both Mussolini and Claretta in a mountain hut in the Dolomites, on Jocherhof Peak at about the 3000 metre elevation, where nobody would bother looking for them. Originally, he had earmarked the hide-out for another prominent person. There had been great opposition from the Vatican against the deportation of Jews from Rome, and Hitler became so enraged that he planned to capture and imprison the Pope. As an ardent Catholic, Franz had designated the refuge for the Holy See; however, Hitler finally relented and the retreat was not needed. It was ready now to receive the Duce. The plan, however, did not materialize; in the turmoil of late April, 1945, with total defeat looming, Mussolini, while attempting to escape, was captured and executed by Italian partisans. The bodies of both the Duce and Claretta were transported to Milan and hanged, with their feet up, for public display. By that time, I had been transferred and had left Lake Garda and Italy.

My assumption about the integrity of Franz Spögler was confirmed; he was a straightforward character, without fault or Nazi fanaticism. After the war, he became a prominent member of the South Tyrolean Peoples Party and served as a member of the legislature for several terms, castigating the Italian government's move to settle 3000 Italian bureaucrats in the German-speaking town of Bolzano. "Bringing in 3000 Italians means 30,000 Italians, with their cooks, their nannies, chauffeurs, gardeners, housekeepers, and their families." Franz wanted to preserve the German language and Tyrolean culture and was active in endorsing a German-language television channel for Tyrolia. He died in 2008, a patriotic zealot, much respected by his community. His previous superior, the Fasano Ambassador Rudolf Rahn, unscathed by the Nuremberg war trials, advanced in his civil activity to a prominent position in business with Coca-Cola in Germany.

Gisela's departure from Fasano seemed to be symbolic of my destiny also. TF1 had been deployed in Italy for over a year; it was now a permanent installation and had outlived its purpose as a mobile military unit. Lt. Holtmann, still our immediate supervisor, was a good leader who treated everyone fairly; nobody was disadvantaged. Politically, he seemed to be abstaining from an opinion; he never spoke about the Nazis or their government in glorifying terms. He knew my personal interests and how I felt about the regime. I could get a feeling about his political conviction; he would not use the expression "Der Führer," but speak of "Hitler" and "The Government." We, his three corporals, Bruno Marzi from Vienna, Austria, Kurt Foeckel from Leipzig, Saxonia, and I from Oldenburg on the North Sea coast, had shared our quarters. In our chess games during the long Russian winter nights we had often put our lieutenant into checkmate. Bruno and Kurt had left as frontline volunteers for the hollow reward of becoming *Der Führer's* officers in the German Reich. Neither was to survive. My choice was not heroism but survival for a better future, and I preferred the more sedate and secure embassy life in Fasano.

For entertainment, even in the land of Vivaldi and Verdi, true cultural benefits for soldiers did not exist. We were occasionally trucked to the nearest town for a German movie or a stage show. Unexpectedly, an enlightening exception arose in the form of a three-day performance by a prominent French string quartet playing classical music at the Hotel Excelsior in Venice. The catch was that the allotment was one ticket only for the entire regiment. Lt. Holtmann put up my name and, I presume, his strong solicitation for me as the recipient. Surprisingly, as a result, of the entire one thousand or so men of the regiment, I was chosen. The experience in Venice was truly edifying. During the performances, the high windows were open to the lagoon's gentle Adriatic zephyr that moved the long curtains while the room filled with the sound of *"L'apres-midi d'un faun," "Clair de lune," "La mer,"* "Pavane for a dead princess," and "The girl with the flaxen hair," all by the composer Claude Debussy who famously described the best part of music as "the silence between the notes."

The Hotel Excelsior on the Lido Beach in Venice where I attended an unforgettable series of Claude Debussy concerts.

When I returned to Fasano, the harmonious tune of "La Mer" still filled by memory. I called to thank Lt. Holtmann and he told me that the cultural treat was his farewell gift; the

Debussy quartets were the swan song for my time with TF1 Company. It was no secret that the days of Hitler's Blitzkriegs were over. TF transmission had lost its usefulness while the attrition of fighting soldiers on the front exceeded the replacement by new recruits. Efforts were made to fill the vacancies with previously non-combatant soldiers such as ourselves. While my two more enthused NCO-comrades, Marzi and Foeckel, lured by the opportunity to become officers for *Der Führer's* final victory, had already left as volunteers, my plans were less epic and more conservative. Lt. Holtmann explained that my position had become untenable under a new quota assessment, that I was to be transferred to become an officer also, and that was an order.

The lieutenant informed me that following the cultural treat in Venice, I was not to return to the embassy in Fasano but to report for duty to an artillery unit on the Gothic Line near Bologna, a tactical military obstruction thrown up against the allied advance north. As a prospective officer cadet, it was my task to prove myself in a month-long period of front-line experience. Arriving at the new destination, I learned that enemy shelling frequently damaged the telephone lines to the German artillery observers, and my assignment was somewhat macabre and ironical. As a "communications specialist," I was picked to crawl out in a ploughed field under enemy fire to repair the field telephone wires shot to pieces by the Canadian artillery across from us. These *Canucks*, however, seemed to have the attitude of "if you don't shoot at us, we'll leave you alone," a type of warfare that suited me just fine. My task was still touch and go because there was sporadic shelling, and the missiles seemed to be directed at me. With a slow-flying spotter plane circling above, I had good reason to fear for my life. If killed, my loss would be perhaps acknowledged as a hero's death, but I did not have a scintilla of patriotic courage in me. Was this the way my father had felt before he returned home as a wounded veteran? Had he been forced to fight, to sacrifice himself against his own will?

Was this how the millions of dead soldiers had been turned into heroes?

Preferring to remain a surviving coward, I soon learned that most of the shells fired, although they struck close by, did not explode, but ended up in the ground with a dull thump. Explosion or not, just as a heavy rock could strike and kill by accident, I feared these lumps of iron could find their target inadvertently, and I took cover. There were quiet intervals that I spent behind bales of straw in a small deserted farmhouse reading old *National Geographic* magazines that the eccentric occupant must have been collecting.

Instead of being inspired with heroism, I managed to survive the artillery fire, completed the tour of duty, and seemed to have demonstrated to my superiors some measure of frontline skills and an aura of courage and intrepidity, enough to qualify as an officer cadet. They rewarded me with a pass for five days' leave at home in Germany and travelling orders for an officers' school at a town in Czechoslovakia, a country in the Greater German Reich. Whether I wanted to or not, the system would pound me into an officer of the *Reich*. I was just as determined to throw a wrench into the gear of the unwanted scheme.

Chapter 10

Although serving as a target for enemy artillery practice had left me with me a good scare, it had caused me no physical harm. The fiery front-line ordeal, while it made me streetwise and aware of the folly of false heroism, had also earned me a five-day leave at home. Mother, illegally, had hoarded food for just such an occasion when one of her three boys might show up. The Grundig radio in the living room allowed me to sample the fruit from the forbidden BBC tree. News tidings reported the progress of the Allied advance since the Normandy invasion, which the German stations could only meekly confirm. Hitler's heyday, when men would volunteer for enlistment to invade other countries, was over. The Führer was too late pointing his "I want YOU!" finger at me to become an officer, to lead men to their death. It was a question of *"Chercher midi a quatorze"* (looking for lunch at fourteen hundred hours), as French Canadians say. It was too late. Hitler was too late. I was not interested. What good would it do? Resisting the invasion would only prolong the agony. "A quick end with terror is better than terror without end." Until that moment of quick terror, every day would count.

My travel papers included the order to report for officer's training at a place called Brno in Czechoslovakia, a country that had been annexed into the Reich in 1939. It was toward the middle of February 1945, when I left Mother. I started on my way reluctantly, taking my time. Nobody could hold me accountable for arriving late as our cities and rail stations were bombed almost regularly, and travel in crowded trains with uncertain schedules and unexpected stops was unpredictable. My route took several days from Oldenburg via Berlin to Dresden where I spent a quiet night sleeping soundly in a warm recess under some stairs at the main station.

The next morning, I checked with the *Wehrmacht Feld Polizei* for rations and revalidation of my travelling papers. The elderly sergeant in charge looked at me. There was compassion in his eyes. He may have seen me as a naïve idealistic young volunteer, misguided and anxious to sacrifice myself for Hitler's final showdown. He had probably sent many so indoctrinated and eager to become officers, with the death warrant in their pockets, on a journey of no return. Determined that I was not going to be one of them, I said nothing. I wanted to put off my engagement at all costs; even a day or two of delay would be a day or two nearer the end of the war.

The sergeant informed me that Brno in Czechoslovakia was no longer available as an officer training centre--the town had changed hands into Russian control, and he was to redirect me to the *Pionier Schule* at Regensburg in Bavaria. Sensing a touch of paternal concern in his questioning, and in view of my relocation to another destination, I took the bold step of asking modestly: "Sir, could I have a few days off, please? My mother is a widow and I am her oldest son." The man took pity on me, unaware or ignoring that I had just completed a five-day leave. He himself may have been worrying about a son somewhere on the front. I could sense that he did not want me to become cannon fodder for an illusory thousand-year Reich. He issued the document that I asked for. The certificate would keep me away from war for five more days; five days closer to the end of the killing.

With revised and freshly-stamped travel papers in my pocket, I was going to take my time. The new itinerary included an extended detour, again from Dresden via Berlin, back to Oldenburg in the extreme north of the country. Five days later, I would get on my way to Regensburg in the far south, all legal and proper according to the papers. Mother was surprised to see me again so soon. Despite being hard of hearing, her radio had, this time without the musical prelude, reported the death of tens of thousands of civilians in a massive air raid on Dresden and its main railroad station, the very place where I had slumbered so peacefully the night before. I had to think of the fate of the fatherly *Wehrmacht* sergeant who had extended my leave, and how close I had come to perish in the bombing.

This time at home, in anticipation of the impending collapse of the Reich, I prepared an emergency escape kit. For identification, it included the German civilian passport I had obtained for my Holland bike journey, and an old road map of the German Automobile Association. Another document was a letter of acknowledgement from Wurzburg University. Although merely a paper of informal registration by mail, should I, after the war, apply for matriculation, the document could appear to the uninformed as evidence that I was a student of medicine. The most precious item in my kit was a new publication, a German pocket textbook entitled *Englisch in 27 Lektionen.* I was surprised to find this book on the shelf of an Oldenburg bookstore at a time of shortage of all materials. How had the publisher managed to put a product of such untimely content on the market? The solution was that he had included a complimentary chapter about the Führer; furthermore, the book cover showed a picture of Adolf Hitler holding the hand of a flower girl in a German ethnic dress. A smart move! The sensitive Nazi press could not resist that literary temptation and had approved the book. Despite the overzealous fanatics searching for enemies of the German Reich, I could openly read this book displaying the Führer's picture, legitimizing my English studies, at the same time demonstrating patriotism!

I thought myself well prepared, having taken part in Naumann's optional English classes and adopted unknowingly some of his awkward Cockney accent. During the final days of the insane nightmare, the twenty-seven lessons were to turn out to be my best investment. Strangely enough, I had no thought of needing food, camping equipment, matches, a pocket knife, or a field flask. My mind was set only on severing my connection with the entire system. As I left Mother at the end of my second sojourn at home, she shook my hand and sent me on my way with a visionary "*Auf Wiedersehen*, son, when we have peace.*" Hugging and kissing were not her way of expressing maternal affection.

The Regensburg *Pionier Schule* for officer cadets was housed in standard military barracks. I enjoyed walking through the old town and remembered the history of the stone bridge across the Danube River. Similar to the Charles Bridge in Prague, the mortar contained all the eggs the country's hens could produce for years; during bridge construction no eggs could be had for other purposes. The structure is of medieval origin and the protein-bound mortar has kept it in good condition. When in our barracks, we trainees were expected to prepare for our future work as leaders of quasi-suicide missions, to study mining plans, prepare effective explosive combinations, and study how to blow up pillboxes by pushing the charge forward on a long two by four. Whenever I could, I withdrew inconspicuously into a corner, trying to avoid provoking the fanatics, and learned by heart all twenty-seven lessons, one at a time, including the one about the Führer. As the others were memorizing land-mining templates and patterns, I became proficient in English. They called me a *Verräter*, a traitor, and reported my activity. I believe that the iconic picture of good Adolf Schicklhuber (our ridiculing nickname for Hitler, allegedly the maiden name of his mother) was my guardian angel. Nothing came of the charges against me.

Our daily march to the training grounds took us past a prison camp that held British soldiers, likely captured air pilots, who, unlike my roommates, would be intelligent men. To my astonishment, I saw their hands shackled and thought that they had committed crimes during their short imprisonment in Germany, however, I learned that their handcuffs were a collective reprisal against a similar measure the British had applied to German prisoners in their raid on Dieppe. To approach the men or assure them of my good will would be a breach of security. They were the enemy behind barbed wire and inaccessible. I wondered about their fate as we marched past almost daily.

At that time, every group of people, even Mother's Methodist congregation, and particularly our bunch of officer candidates, had fanatics among them who still believed that Germany was going to win the war. They spoke of new, secret developments such as the "V 2 and V 3" weapons, rumours of which we had already heard back during my *Arbeits Dienst* service, weapons that would change the course of the war at the last minute. The "V" was the initial letter of *Vergeltung*, vengeance. What there was to be avenged remained unclear since it was Germany who had started this war and bombed British cities first. Perhaps it meant revenge for the unfair Treaty of Versailles? Despite the boasted new weapons, nothing unusual happened; the weeks went; the American advance closed in on us inexorably.

I counted the days the Americans would take to reach Regensburg and had made my own plan to deal with the decisive moment. As a non-smoker, I had traded every package of my Reemtsma cigarette ration for a chocolate package called Schokakola, which contained caffeine and some cola as a stimulant. Although I had accumulated a good amount of this non-perishable food for my journey, I was uncertain how long it would sustain me while I attempted to gain my freedom. Conversely, should things go awry, my fate could be that of the thousands of Russian prisoners we had observed starving to death near Pskow. There was no point being sensitive about the final showdown, whether sublime or devastating. Those radio stations still under German control continued to fanfare the broadcast announcements by the same Franz Liszt *Preludes* that had set the listeners' minds on victory at the beginning. However, in the expectation of the impending fall, the melody now sounded hollow.

When the American advance was reported to have reached Nuremberg from the north, we moved out of Regensburg to avoid civilian casualties from bombing raids on the historic town and found quarters in the school of a small nearby village. On April 12, 1945, we heard over our military radio that President Roosevelt had died. I hoped that this historic event would have some influence on the course of the war, but the hostilities continued. There was one incident, however, that may or may not have been a consequence of Roosevelt's passing. During one of our endurance marches in the country, we were taking a roadside rest when a strange apparition approached. A loose column of very slow-moving humans, all dressed in striped garments and caps, obviously prisoners without baggage or equipment, shuffled past us, barefoot in wooden clogs. They were men of indeterminable age, staggering corpses of anywhere between twenty and seventy years, emaciated, tanned and mute, their faces expressionless. They made no eye contact, showed no interest in us, did not even look in our direction. They did not ask for food; they just stumbled forward, staggered, staring straight ahead. One solitary guard, an elderly soldier, obviously of the Reserves, wearing a long warm grey coat in contrast to the thin prison stripes, armed with an outdated '88 army rifle on his back, kept his distance from them, walking equally slowly, patiently, as though he, the caretaker, felt empathy for his impaired charges. And then they were gone.

I had heard of the term *Musselman* in connection with concentration camp internees, humans so exhausted, starved, and humiliated, so apathetic and listless, that they become unapproachable and assume a prone position similar to the Mussulman's (Muslim's) attitude of prayer. I have learned nothing since to explain the reason for the appearance of this procession of human misery on a highway north of Regensburg other than that it took place a few days after

Roosevelt's passing. It is possible that a camp *Kommandant*, anticipating the approaching final judgement, had a last-minute stirring of conscience or guilt and tried to mitigate his accountability after the war by pretending to have taken humanitarian measures for these people. He may have tried to improve their condition by putting them into intact, clean-looking prison uniforms, probably the only means of improvement available, and transferring them to a "better" concentration camp. They did not appear to be in any other ameliorated condition. There was no evidence of addressing their need to fend off starvation; no horse-drawn field kitchen followed them. They were gone as they had come.

This was my sole brief encounter with concentration camp inmates. At the time, to a man, we officer cadets did not know what to make of them. Instead of empathy, we felt repulsed; the feelings, which the sight of this wraith created amongst us, were almost of hostility. At the time, we did not wonder why such sentiments were aroused in us. Why did not we, like the Reservist guard, feel empathy toward fellow human beings? Were we afraid that we might see mirrored in these abject spectres an image of our own coming prostration, surrender, defeat, which we were not yet ready to accept or to embrace? A defeat from which, in a few short hours or days, we ourselves would literally be fleeing?

As a deterrent against desertion, stories were put into circulation within our company that defectors had been caught and hanged on the nearest lamppost. While the rumours put fear into me, they also stimulated fresh ideas, indicating that the general enthusiasm for the Reich was waning. My careful inquiries revealed two other like-minded comrades sharing the misfortune to be commandeered to the officer cadet school. We discussed what we could do and laid out a plan of action.

Within a few days, the American spearhead was reported fifteen kilometres north of Regensburg. We were assigned defensive positions on the ridge of a rocky outcrop. A highway below was hemmed in by the rock wall on one side and a swampy river on the other, an ideal location for an ambush. Weapons were issued; I was not interested in defending Nazi Germany nor was I going to begin fighting World War II just as it ended. I needed a weapon not directed against the invaders but strictly for self-defence against those who would interfere with my plan to regain my freedom. The standard infantry weapon issued was the "Karabiner 98," the rifle of my outstanding results during target practice, which had earned me my first three-day leave. This time, however, I succeeded in obtaining just what I needed, an automatic "Model 43" gun that, in contrast to the regular military carbine, would spread bursts of ten rounds at a time. It was firepower I wanted, and at close range; I had my unspoken reason for this choice.

We dug our foxholes as best we could among the shrubs on the ridge of the rock elevation and waited. Each of us had been issued a *panzer faust*, an anti-tank bazooka, a heavy, cumbersome piece to carry. So, there I sat in my hole with the treasure of an automatic rifle across my knees, and ammunition, and the nonsensical anti-tank bazooka, and in my knapsack several cans of *Schokakola*, my civilian passport, and the Automobile Club road map. My soldier's pay book was hidden in my sock; if it came to a showdown, I did not want to be taken for SS and shot; I would have proof that I was only a regular German soldier. As an afterthought, although I thought it ridiculous, I had included a clean, white handkerchief in a waterproof cloth.

Quite unexpectedly, there was small arms fire from below; the bullets zinged around me like whip cracks but much louder. I ducked into my foxhole, never having experienced such personal insult before except for the impotent artillery shelling on my last assignment in Italy. Then there was a very loud bang somewhere below. As I peered over the edge, I saw an American Jeep on fire, stopped halfway across the road, the driver and front passenger slumped forward and obviously dead. It must have been the result of one of our *panzer fausts*. Unreal. I heard one of my comrades yelling in a frenzy of excitement: "I've hit one of them, I've hit one!" He repeated himself, boasting his success several times. He was euphoric beyond reason, temporarily demented, I thought. The Jeep had not been attacking him; it was merely driving down the road. Why would he do such a thing? He had been one of the most fanatic objectors critical of my English studies. I offered him my *panzer faust*, and he greedily grabbed it with both hands and crept forward again, trying his luck once more as if he were in a shooting gallery. I was rid of the offensive weapon, glad I would not have to leave incriminating evidence behind.

My two loyal friends came crawling to the edge of my hole and asked: "Do you think the time has come?" With those bullets whistling around, I most definitely agreed. We cautiously withdrew to the back. We had rehearsed what to say and what to do in case of interference. With the automatic rifle in the crook of my arm, the safety switch off, my finger on the trigger, we climbed down the rear of the rocky hill. If a fanatic were to challenge us, we would first pretend that we wanted to cover another small isolated rock against the enemy. If the person questioning us were an officer, and if he aimed his pistol at us, I was emotionally prepared. From my school years, I remembered the ethical teachings of the philosopher Emmanuel Kant. I would obey Kant's categorical imperative, as I understood the dogma, to survive; I would have the advantage of surprise, pulling the trigger before he did, and I would expend all ten shots. The intruder would be a dead man; it would be self-defense. And so we left. It was to our good fortune that nobody interfered; all were busy fighting the Americans on the other side of the rocks, prolonging the war.

We three stepped down on open farmland and went for a small depression filled with a dense grove of trees, a good hiding place. When we reached the spot, all was quiet; we sat down and took council in our new location. We caught a

Gerd Asche

glimpse over the edge of our hide-out and saw in the distance a long column of American tanks, with infantry on top, moving across the land, parallel to the patrol which had run into our ambush. The small action in our area would be over shortly; we had to move north as soon as we could to avoid being caught in the encirclement. We waited until dark; I looked at my rifle; I never had to use it and realized that during the entire war I never had ever fired a single shot against any person. I removed the chamber and magazine and threw them away in one direction and the rifle in another. They may still be where I left them sixty-five years ago.

We had made the break. If captured now, it no longer meant an on-the-spot court martial and hanging. The worst outcome would be an American prisoner-of-war camp, which was said to be reasonably humane. So far, we were free, carrying no weapons, equipped only with our essentials of survival. Some unusual thoughts entered my conscience about our legal status. Where did we fit into international prisoner-of-war conventions? Were we still German nationals? We had left German Nazi jurisdiction, yet, officially, we were not under American law. We were stateless, belonging to nobody, legally responsible to nobody, and nobody was responsible for us. The old laws no longer applied and yet a new law, in a sense the opposite, did not rule us; we were in a legal no-man's-land, having thrust ourselves out of civilized society into a state of nature, a mini-society of our own.

Our German army uniforms made us highly visible; we could move only at night. In the dark, we stumbled into a camp of American tanks and their crew who, fortunately, had no sentinel and no dogs and were all fast asleep. We cautiously tip-toed out again. Another night when vision was poor, I led our group along a narrow forest trail. I tripped over an obstruction and fell. We identified the hitch as a dead Luftwaffe soldier lying across the trail. We did not take time to investigate the drama of an airman's lonely death in the

Bavarian forest. We realized that night-walking was a poor way to move; our progress was discouraging.

At daybreak, we reached an area without recent military action. When we noted some farm workers a ways off in the fields, we decided to risk the more efficient daylight travel. Assuming that from a distance we could perhaps be taken for farmers, we set out across the open country. Soon, however, we ran into an impasse in the form of a busy highway that seemed to be a military supply route. Vehicle followed vehicle while we cowered in the roadside bushes waiting for a break in traffic. Since running or moving fast would have made us more conspicuous, we decided, should the best opportunity arise, to walk quite leisurely across the road, pretending to be farmers. (Imagine our naivety, a bunch of three young German soldiers in their uniforms, expecting to be taken for farmers!) We had barely reached the centre of the road in an ostensibly leisurely walk when we heard a vehicle approach. Our steps became faster and faster. By the time the occupants of the oncoming Jeep saw us, we were no longer innocent farmers but three fleeing German soldiers. We reached the other side and hid behind a low bush.

The Jeep travelled another hundred yards and came to a screeching halt. An American soldier jumped out and ran toward us. He stopped, raised his automatic pistol, and fired a burst of shots in our direction. At that moment, I recalled my childhood literature about Americans, about the fair play of the romantic hero of Cooper's Leatherstocking tales. I felt very sure of myself and knew what to do. Determined to resolve the situation, I advised my two companions to run for their freedom while I rose from behind the bush, stood as tall as I could, unwrapped my white handkerchief, and waved it high in an arc left to right, shouting, as I had learned from my English textbook, "I surrender, I surrender!" In my unfamiliarity with the expression, I pronounced the word "surrender" incorrectly, with the emphasis on the the first syllable, the "sur."

I do not think I ever shall know if the course of events following was pure synchronicity or the workings of divine function. Such things are among the great mysteries of life. I should claim it proved the presence of God and the adulation that He was good. However, I am not a mystic; my life experience suggests to me that beyond human thought and comprehension lies a cosmic utility forming, together with coincidence and misfortune, the engine of our human destiny and our individual and petty existences. Regardless of the faulty enunciation of the word "surrender," the American soldier seemed to accept my capitulation. He slung his rifle over his shoulder and walked in my direction. Halfway, he halted, bent down, and lifted up a rabbit or hare that he had shot. With the prey in his hand, he turned, got into the Jeep and drove off, completely ignoring my capitulation and me.

We felt good about our salvation; however, the American had shown us our true worth. Being one of three young Germans, ignored in preference of a dead rabbit, did not encourage great expectations about our future. I became convinced and confident, almost "cocky," however, that nothing serious would happen to me on our precarious adventure. We realized, though, that one factor impeded our progress more than the lack of food, the need for sleep, or the want of shelter against rain. What was slowing us down was the conspicuousness of our uniforms. We had to be continuously on guard against surprises. We had ripped off all incriminating insignia; there was no longer a swastika on our tunics or on our belt buckles but we could see no way to change our garments. If we could only get rid of those grey coats! We felt that civilian clothes would be the solution, allowing us to move on the roads during daytime. We did not realize, however, that the appearance of a group of three young transients of military age, whether in uniforms or as civilians, would tell the story as clearly as the nose in our face.

Our fortune seemed to change when we came unexpectedly upon a straight waterway. From my road map, we identified it as the Ludwig Kanal. I remembered from teacher Dannemann's geography and history class that the Bavarian king had built a canal during the Industrial Revolution with the grandiose idea of joining Russia's Black Sea via the Danube, the Main, and the Rhine rivers, to the Dutch seaport of Rotterdam and thus obtain access to the North Sea and the Atlantic Ocean. It was the waterway Hitler had envisioned as the route to transport Black Sea oil into central Europe. Although the original project proved disappointing to the Bavarian king and was never executed by the Germans, to us fugitives the old tow trail along the Kanal appeared promising. There was no boat or barge traffic, and the narrow tow horse trail that precluded motor vehicle traffic kept us safe from American military patrols.

We continued north along the waterway and saw a young fellow fishing from the wall of one of the many locks; he was chewing gum and smoking a foreign cigarette from a red package imprinted Pall Mall. Judging by his accent, he was a *Fremd Arbeiter*, one of the foreign workers on whom the local agriculture and farming depended. These people would, shortly after the war, become known as D.P.s, displaced persons, doing the work of the German men who were killed in battle or held as prisoners of war. Our new acquaintance seemed surprisingly friendly and willing to help us on our way. I made him understand that we wanted to get rid of our incriminating uniforms and asked him: "Could you get us some civilian clothes in exchange?" The young man said he would help and provide each of us with a suit of clothing. It seemed too good to be true, to have the opportunity to get the coveted civilian clothes and be able to move more freely. However, how would this foreign worker in Germany have ready access to three sets of men's wear in the fifth year of war when there was strict rationing of clothes? Even though the trade offered a good deal for the lad in view of the better quality of the uniform material, I half-suspected a trap, but we were fugitives without options. We followed him into the village where he took us to his room in the farm building. Lo and behold, if he did not come up with three sets of used pants, shirts, and jackets. While we changed, he congratulated us, ironically; it was April 20, Adolf Hitler's birthday.

While tugging on our pants, we heard car noises; indeed, an American patrol was arriving. I made sure all my documents, the pay book, the road map, and the letter from Würzburg University were transferred into the new pockets. Barely closing my trousers, holding shirt and jacket under my arm, I ran into the bushes at the back and hid, assuming that my comrades had acted similarly. The fellow was true to his word; he did not give us away but went to the front of the house, received the patrol, and waved them off in a different direction. I could tell by the way he pointed while I was running.

Once outside the village, putting on the shirt and coat and fastening my trousers, I discovered important buttons missing. On this evening of my conversion to civilian status, I crawled deep into a haystack. Stories flashed in my mind, of fugitives hiding in stacks of straw discovered by sabres or bayonets stuck into the pile. While these weapons were no longer used, a round from the machine pistol fired into the hay would get me. However, everything remained quiet. Nobody came for me; I must have fallen asleep. It was dark. A solitary gunshot in the distance woke me up, and then another, and all became quiet again. Not a dog barked; not a cow mooed.

It was an eerie, moonless night, full of silent danger. I crawled out of the hay and cautiously called my companions several times but heard nothing. I dared not return to the house; not all American patrols were benign Natty Bumppos; they may have been waiting to spend the third bullet on me. My two comrades, now in civilian clothes, if not captured, may have been shot in the dark as marauding partisans. I never saw either of them again. I forgot their names and do not know if the two shots I heard had been for them. If they survived, and if we had remained a group of three, even out of the uniforms, we would still have had a difficult time. American patrols could have mistaken us for partisans or brigands, free game for any legitimate army. We had been emboldened when one soldier ignored us in favour of wild game but we could not expect the same indifference from a patrol entering the village on the Ludwig's Kanal. They may have had different ideas about roaming enemy members, particularly if disguised in civilian rags. They could have taken us for SS fanatics. My two companions may have saved my life by losing theirs.

As a lone fugitive I had the advantage of finding food and obtaining shelter more easily, and with my recently improved English, I could better convince the authorities that I was a non-combatant. Now that I was alone, I recognized how foolhardy our joint venture had been. The safest way for all of us to survive legitimately would have been to surrender and become prisoners of war. However, these considerations paled in the light of the urge to get home.

My civilian clothes were actual rags; the pants were thin and offered no protection when I had to sleep outdoors. The worst part about them was the fact that the seam in the crotch was ripped from front to back so that I had to walk with a defined gait, keeping my legs together in order to preserve my decency. All the same, wearing them felt much more comfortable, almost legitimate. I was now quite alone. Continuing my trek along the canal, I reached northern Bavaria, just short of Nuremberg, where the waterway passes through a settlement of small gardens and outbuildings called Schreber Gärten. Although the buildings were improvised shacks, many had become permanent residences because the regular homes in the city had been bombed during the air raids on Nuremberg. I approached an obviously retired gentleman leaning contentedly on the garden fence. One word led to the next and he invited me in and made me comfortable to stay the night. After a warm meal as decent as my host could serve a guest under the prevailing circumstances, a plateful of pan-fried potatoes,

Gerd Asche

I revealed my plans to become a physician. My host confided that he was a surviving German underground Communist and pointed out that, although of a different social class, he respected me as sharing his anti-Nazi sentiments. For the night, I laid down on the wooden floor and had a wonderful sleep under a solid roof after many nights in the open.

Although the military drills had made me used to endurance marching, the present rapid advance on my own was more demanding; I had developed swollen ankles from continuous walking on the hard road surface. However, the joints were not painful and I could continue. On my advance north, I avoided the Autobahn freeways. There would be heavy military traffic and besides, they ended up nowhere, circling or bypassing towns without offering any chance to meet people. Travelling secondary roads would lead to small villages or towns with access to food, shelter, and information.

By now, I had reached deep behind the advancing occupation lines and a threat from American patrols seemed no longer a factor. Being rid of my uniform reduced my anxiety. I wanted to get home badly and dared taking to the road openly. Before I reached the town of Bamberg, however, an American Jeep patrol stopped me and requested documents. How serendipitous to have on me my certificate of registration for the nearby Würzburg University! My way out was to claim that I wanted to resume my medical studies. Despite my questionable attire, it could be plausible to an uninitiated stranger that I was an indigent student on my way to the university. Together with my civilian passport, my military pay book hidden in my sock, the student document seemed proof that I was not a soldier or a suspect and, after questioning, they let me go. My command of the *27 Lessons in English* must have helped in alleviating their suspicion.

Two days later I reached the junction of the Ludwig's Canal with the Main River. A farmer allowed me to share dinner with his large family. The food was simple; we all helped ourselves out of a large earthen mug to the white wine produced in the Main River region. It was part of good table manners, observed by everyone, to wipe your mouth before taking a swig from the jug. For the night, they allowed me in the hayloft. The favourable outcome of the encounter with the American patrol had raised my self-confidence. Well rested, I continued my journey, through Hesse into Westphalia, finally striking the banks of the familiar Weser River and feeling that I was getting closer to home. Past the town of Höxter, the road was empty of traffic or people until I caught up with a woman having a difficult time carrying a load of dry wood she had collected. I took the burden off her shoulders, and she explained that she lived in the small village ahead, called Nachtigall, nightingale, and when I remarked on the unusual name of the place, she said she had lived there all her life and had been content with the name. She even would not mind to have Hitler back. The problem, she complained bitterly, was the soldiers who had taken over the village. They were Belgian occupation troops; they had impounded everything portable and movable, from sewing machines, radios, furniture, bicycles, handcarts, wagons, and boats, to their horses and oxen, including their cars and trucks. They had even recruited young girls as "domestic helpers." No, things had been better under Hitler, and now she had to go out on foot to pick firewood to cook her meals. Her appearance, an old woman carrying a bundle of wood, reminded me of pictures in fairy tale books, indicating hopeless abject poverty.

We approached the small school building where the soldiers were quartered. The lady warned me again of the Belgians' notoriety in the treatment of prisoners of war, that they were unpredictable, "worse than the French," she added. She did not elaborate, nor did I ask for details. I had heard rumours of French fanatics dropping railroad ties from overpasses onto the open boxcars filled with German prisoners of war as their train passed below them. Getting so much closer to my own home and wanting to avoid capture at all costs, I asked for her advice about bypassing Nachtigall by proceeding along the mountain ridge. "Don't go that way!" she warned. "That choice is worse than taking on the Belgians; there are still remnants of SS in the hills."

The topography restricted my choices to three options. To my right, I could see the Weser River flowing north. It was May; the water was still too cold to swim and there were no vessels in which to cross; all boats had been seized. Continuing north on the road where we stood would expose me to the feared Belgians. Lastly, to my left, the hills were contaminated with SS who might recruit me to join them. I was in a situation I had not faced before, marked by a senseless, disorienting, surreal distortion of impending danger, of losing my freedom. I was desperate and made a desperate decision. I would go directly into the village, into the lion's den of the occupying Belgian soldiers, and innocently ask for help.

Unaware of what my immediate future would be, I am left to consider that what followed was pure coincidence or the workings of providence. The strange outcome of my decision was not revealed immediately, but my life experience suggests to me that beyond human thought and comprehension lies a cosmic order. Entering the lions lair was not rational and beyond my conscious decision. Paradoxically, it proved to be one of the most propitious moves I would make.

We had reached the entrance to the school, and I went inside. I found myself in the guard room and in my best Gymnasium-learned French addressed the soldier on duty: *"Bon jour, Monsieur, est ce que je pouvrai parler au Monsieur l'officier?"* The guard, obviously amused at my poor French and its enunciation with a German accent, responded in fluid German and ordered me to enter. A body search revealed my military pay book hidden in my sock. "Aha," the NCO exclaimed gloatingly, "here we have the *Unter Offizier* Gerd Asche!" Fortunately, the entry of my simple rank had not been changed to officer cadet. They kept me and treated me quite reasonably for my low rank, even with preference, as I found later. One of them, about my age, asked me to join him for his meal, which was issued in the school auditorium. This room also contained a stage with several beds. I was quite surprised to find them occupied by Belgian soldiers tucked in, side by side, with young girls of the village. As far as I perceived, they were merely lying in bed together, not embracing, not hugging, nor did I see sexual activity, although this was obviously why they had the girls in their beds. They all ignored me; what took place on stage went on without regard for modesty, without care about my presence. My memory returned to the American soldier's rabbit hunt as I realized that the lost war had brought me into this situation of loss of identity. How unimportant had my number become! The uncertainty about my immediate future, of which freedom was the first concern, precluded any other interests, but the unreal, almost phantasmal Kafkaesque circumstances were crushing my self-esteem. A real-life situation had changed into a genre, which was incomprehensibly complex and uncanny. I made a mental note: should I ever write of my experience in the school gymnasium of the enticingly-named village of Nachtigall, the reader might reject the bizarre stage scene as unrealistic fiction.

My new Belgian friend and I spent the evening together talking. At bedtime, however, he requested me to proceed to the lockup where, to my surprise, six or eight German soldiers in their proper intact army uniforms were kept on straw. Wearing only rags, I became aware of my preferred treatment, for which, to this day, I have no explanation. On my way to the cell, I made a mental note of a large number of bicycles standing in the basement, obviously requisitioned locally and not used. The other German prisoners had been treated quite humanely. Nobody complained; they had been fed well. My Belgian friend and jailer told me that tomorrow they would take us for interrogation to the American military police in Höxter, the town I had bypassed on foot that morning. My resentment against the Belgians began to soften.

The next morning, a small truck took us to the Höxter prison building, and we were herded into the front hall. I had received back my pay book and was anxious to get rid of its incriminating evidence. I requested to be escorted to the toilet where I was left alone. With the door locked, I tore up the booklet and flushed it down. Soon we were called, one by one, before the officer in charge, an American, Captain Beuer. My twenty-seven lessons in English must have been effective. Despite my ragged attire, the officer took the story well when I presented my questionable documentation of the matriculation at Würzburg University and accepted my claim that I was a medical student, about to return to my studies. He regretted, almost apologized, that at the present time travel was restricted. He made the sensible decision that, as a medical man, I should work in the local hospital until the situation was stable and that he would arrange for my employment. He then discharged me, completing and handing me a small printed card certifying that I was not to be classified as a prisoner of war. It was my passport to freedom.

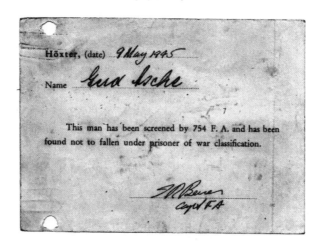

Despite its grammatical flaw, the certificate issued by US
Captain Beuer was my priceless ticket to freedom.

With the invaluable document in my hand, I walked out of the prison a free man. I did not care that the certificate's grammar was a bit thin, although correct English would have increased the credibility and my legal status as a citizen in occupied Germany. During the interview I was unaware that the German armistice had been signed on the day before, nor could I say whether the American officer knew about it. Regardless of its possible effect on my freedom of action, I ignored the instruction to remain in Höxter and immediately set out again on foot toward the village with the Belgian occupation. Captain Beuer's ticket had put my life together again. No longer was I a stateless indefinable individual; neither a combatant, nor a prisoner of war, I had regained my legitimacy as a citizen and despite my questionable attire marched on in full confidence. As I entered Nachtigall, civilians told me that there had been a change in military personnel. My thoughts went to the bicycles in the school cellar. I entered the school compound again. Presenting my new certificate, I modestly asked the corporal in charge, this time in German: "Could I please have my bicycle from the basement?" The new guard, of course, knew nothing about my previous detention and whether I had been captured with or without a bicycle. He gave me permission to go and get the object I claimed. Looking at the pile of bikes, I feared that some might be the soldiers' property and had the presence of mind to return empty-handed: "I can't find it, Sir; would you allow me to take another bike instead?" There was no objection, and with the unique *carte blanche* opportunity, I took the best I could find.

A mere three hours of pedaling along the left bank of the Weser River took me to the town of Hameln of Pied Piper fame where the receding Germans had outright stupidly blown up the Weser Bridge, using the technique of destruction taught at the Regensburg *Pionier Schule*. However, they had made a bad job of it--the bridge was still passable to foot traffic and, by the grace of Captain Beuer's certificate, I passed the British military checkpoint and officially, entered the British Zone of Occupation. The bike helped enormously; it took me

Gerd Asche

past the town of Minden and the Arminius monument near the site of the German victory over the Roman invaders that I had visited two decades before with my handicapped father. No longer an innocent child and tourist, no more a fleeing fugitive, but a legitimized citizen in my own country, biking the previous route home felt like flying, and the distance to Oldenburg diminished rapidly. Leaving behind the last mountain range, the Porta Westfalica, I entered the plains of Lower Saxony, all flat country down to the North Sea, ideal for bicycling. After a mere two more days, I knocked at Mother's door.

It had taken me twenty-nine days, almost all of them on foot, overcoming obstacles, obstructions, and the obscurity of darkness and temporary loss of identity, to get from Regensburg in Bavaria to Oldenburg near the coast, comparable to a much less precarious walk from Vancouver to Calgary. Left behind were the nightmare of Hitler and his paladins Himmler, Heydrich, of Goering and Goebbels, the persons symbolic of dying for the lost cause of a thousand-year Reich. My swollen ankles troubled me for a few days, but that problem soon subsided. I was alive, I was home before my twenty-fifth birthday, with useful skills, with documents guaranteeing my freedom and pointing me towards a promising future.

Chapter 11

Whether victorious or defeated, the residents at Bremer Strasse 27 did no longer care that Germany had lost the war. They were relieved. No longer would the air warden pry around the back of the house to ensure that all windows were covered and not the smallest beam of light could get out. No longer would the shrill wailing of the sirens have Mother and her tenants leave their warm feather beds in the middle of night to climb down the rickety stairs into the cold, moist cellar. Long white fingers of light no longer probed the night sky for enemy airplanes. Henni Helms felt good about the change for Hertha's sake. They could sleep safely now. No longer would the sound of bombs or anti-aircraft guns trigger an epileptic grand mal seizure in her sister with Down's Syndrome. Hertha would become quite incontinent, down in the cold candlelit cellar among the potatoes, carefully-hoarded coal briquettes, and jars of saccharine-sweetened preserves. Her tongue showed large scars from biting it during convulsions. Henni had tried Phenobarbital but it made Hertha so sleepy that, at the all-clear signal, the three women--Mother, Fräulein Nischewski, and Henni--had to heave Hertha's limp body up the two flights of stairs. The best prevention had been a wooden spoon, eased gently between her clenched teeth during an air raid. Now, with peace in the country, the seizures were less severe. Henni had another reason to rejoice: the Nazi government was no more, and no longer would the Party's health worker snoop on Hertha's condition, on whether she was a candidate for transfer to a "home" where they would "put her to sleep, as an unnecessary consumer of food."

With the cessation of hostilities, the car and truck head-lights were bright again without their slotted covers, and streetlights were on at night. I became used to wearing civilian clothes and my long Brunssen raincoat. The end of the war, however, did not stop the food shortage. Although bread could be had at the baker's now, it was a new type, the only kind there was. It had to be sliced thick because it fell apart easily; it was coarse, crumbly, and without taste, made of imported corn meal. Lining up for the monthly ration coupons continued, however, and that included the need for a ration card for my food allowance once I had arrived home.

Onkel Eduard, Mother's brother, was a heavy smoker and had died from a lung abscess; he had been buried by the time I got home. We would miss his Friday night visits and the flat, oval tin of canned herrings he contributed to our evening meal while he lambasted our so-called Führer. I had learned of the sad end of Henk Scholtens in Groningen. The death of this innocent friend who, in his admiration for the new order, had joined the Dutch SS and perished, struck me badly. And we worried about the fate of my brothers Werner and Kurt who had written last from the Baltic and the northern Russian fronts. What would happen to them if they ended up as prisoners of war under the Russians, the worst fate that could befall them?

Some things changed dramatically. Hitler's enmeshed war industry, which had been running in high gear, had come to an abrupt halt. Many workers lost their jobs and the ranks of the unemployed were swelled by the number of returning war veterans. Gasoline shortage kept the cars off the streets; the town was much quieter. My friend Georg Steinkamp had made it home from nearby Bremen where his ingenuity had kept him comfortably away from soldiering. He had invented a method of aluminizing surfaces into high quality mirrors, producing convex, concave, or parabolic reflectors used in numerous military applications, such as in the radar location of enemy aircraft in the dark. With the change to peace,

Georg had quickly adapted, switching from technical military applications to linguistics. As he spoke English fluently, he now served the British administration as an interpreter and liaison officer with the provisional local German government, his altruistic way of restoring our racked and ruined country. And so it was again Georg on whose advice I counted after my return.

As the universities were still closed, I asked him how I could find employment and do something useful during the interim, and he recommended that I apply for a position corresponding to his, as an interpreter for the Department of Food and Agriculture under the British Control Commission. There was, however, a hitch in entering employment with the British occupation forces, and it did not concern my questionable language skills. I could have begun to work on the same day were it not for the screening of my past political activities. It felt paradoxical; we had just left behind a decade when our well-being, nay, survival, depended on showing our sympathy with, or at least tacit acceptance of, the Nazi regime. Now, the table had turned: obtaining a job depended on the evidence that this was not so, that the opposite applied, that we had been against the Nazis. When my past was scrutinized, however, I was "vetted" and hired. And they kept me on, although they could have had more competent people. It was not so much for my knowledge of English (that was restricted to the contents of the Führer-approved twenty-seven lessons), but because my interpretations made their negotiations easier. I placed less importance on verbatim translation of the word and used expressions that steered problems toward their resolutions, a transgression of which only I was aware, of course. In the eyes of the British I could understand enough of their language to convey its meaning to the German official, Herr Reese, who accepted my presentations because through me, he could, no matter how poorly (he would never know how poorly at the start), communicate with the British.

The British officer in charge of the Regional Food Administration was Colonel Gilbert, middle-aged, affable, a good-looking mustachioed, reddish-blond Anglo-Saxon of tall, aristocratic bearing, smoking expensive Players cigarettes. His secretary, a German *fräulein,* was soon replaced by a tall, short-haired blonde, not unattractive, English woman. She was assigned a car and a British driver and, shortly after, seemed to have quasi moved in with the Colonel in his residence on Garten Strasse. Working under Colonel Gilbert was Major McCharles from Canada who treated me more as an equal than a defeated enemy and told me of his family and his brother, a medical doctor, practicing in a place with the incomprehensible name of Medicine Hat, Alberta. Major McCharles's second-in-command was a French-speaking captain from Moncton, whose name I forget. The two officers had in their entourage a Canadian private soldier. This elderly bachelor, although insignificant, if not useless in his military rank and performance, was a person of marked peculiarities. In his civilian life a postal clerk from Montreal, Henry Duval was a character. He spoke French better than English. In fact, it was outright painful to hear him speak his fractured English; in a conversation he would combine the two languages into one, with a prevailing French pronunciation. Although almost unintelligible, he spoke quite freely, like an orator who thinks he is well understood, and he was not hindered by a short-ness of vocabulary in either language.

Henry told me that he had been transferred from Aldershot, Hampshire, a town in England that had served as a training and drilling ground and accommodation for the Canadian troops. Henry used strong invectives criticizing the British whom he called limeys. During his time in the camp there had been riots of dissatisfaction with their treatment. The dis-content arose from the poor quality of accommodation, the priority given to Americans for returning home, the quality of the food, and the fleecing of Canadian servicemen by local shopkeepers. The anger had led to an uprising with broken windows, ankle-deep glass shards in some places, and over-turned cars. The rebellion had started when a regulation was issued that concerned the goods purchased by the Canadian soldiers to take home as gifts. The people of Britain were short of bicycles, toasters, irons, vacuum cleaners, hair dryers, and electric coffee makers themselves, and a military directive was now forbidding their export to Canada. The goods must be left behind. I could perceive the indignation when Henry, a soldier, member of the force occupying my country, criticized his allies so severely. But then I realized that his berating contained French anti-British undertones originating from a Francophile or Francophone against Anglophones.

Henry never explained the reason for his selective transfer out of Aldershot to Germany instead of being sent straight home to Montreal. He would not have been a person capable of inciting violence; however, it may well have been his offensive English-French rhetoric that drove his superiors to get rid of him as an agitator, a troublemaker. Moving him to Oldenburg had put him on the sidetrack; he worked as a clerk, did a little typing, but was not a member of the food team conferences. His *forte* was the black market where he would trade food and cigarettes, the going currency at the time in the British Zone of Occupation, against German jew-ellery or gold. He once showed me a cartoon drawing that appeared in a British military newspaper and explained its swipe against the poor quality of the British army-issue ciga-rettes. The drawing depicted an unhappy allied soldier, his shoulder patch bearing the letters BAOR (British Army of the Rhine), walking arm-in-arm with an unattractive girl, with the bystander remarking: "What did you expect for Woodbines? Lana Turner?" All knew that cigarettes were the currency used to acquire German goods and services, and there was no misunderstanding about the inferiority of Woodbines. Conversely, the actress Lana Turner was renowned for her physical-sexual attractiveness. I was a non-smoker and never tried Woodbines. Neither my brother Kurt who later joined me at the Food Office, nor I myself ever had problems with Henry. As a Francophone he had made no friends among English-speaking comrades and was probably lonesome. To us he always appeared quite jovial and generous. He had won Mother's heart with a half pound of real coffee.

My work as a translator improved after a few weeks of "teething troubles." I was embarrassed during the initial conferences; the acronym "E.L." puzzled me. I thought that "E.L." might be a common English word. However, I could not find it in Cassell's English-German dictionary and did not want to expose my ignorance by asking for its meaning. It was Henry Duval who found out that "E.L." stood for "essential label," to mark and license agricultural motor vehicles of vital function. I still have the dictionary which could not help me with exotic acronyms, left me by Major McCharles when he returned to Canada.

It was a joyous moment when my youngest brother Kurt walked in. His way to freedom had been shorter but no less dangerous than my own. After the armistice, the Russians had encircled his army group in Courland against the Baltic Sea where the defeated Germans had formed a bridgehead with its back against the water, and almost all of the soldiers and civilian refugee women and children crammed into two giant ocean-going barges with standing room only, and a tug had pulled the vessels out to sea toward German Schleswig-Holstein, along the Russian-occupied coast. An enemy submarine had surfaced and, despite the cease-fire agreement, shelled them and launched a torpedo, albeit without causing loss of life. They reached the small port of Eckernforde in the British Zone of Occupation. Since Kurt's quality of conversational English was superior to mine, Colonel Gilbert took him as a translator until the University of Karlsruhe admitted him as an architect student.

In the mornings, to get to my workplace at the food administration office, I rode the very bike that had carried me home out of Belgian captivity in the village of Nachtigall near

Höxter. Now I pedaled from our house on Bremer Strasse in the east of the city across the Weser-Ems Kanal Bridge, past the State Library and the Natural History Museum, a building, which houses a collection of *Moor Leichen*, moor corpses. Since my school days, I had wondered at the display of the leathery shrunken body of "The Boy of Kayhausen," the preserved corpse of a six-year-old boy discovered in 1922, displayed in a glass tank. Examiners had found that he last ate some millet and sorrel, and his abdominal wall was torn as the result, researchers believe, of a blow. The hip is crooked, a condition known as a congenitally dislocated hip, and the boy apparently had a heavy limp. The historian Tacitus reports that a noticeably large number of moor corpses had physical disabilities. Another bog find revealed the remains of the sixteen-year-old "Girl of Yde" who had suffered from abnormal curvature of the spine. These objects, therefore, had always made the museum a landmark to me.

My bike ride to work continued past the Brunssen Rainwear store, past the Finance Ministry from where I could see the attractive Oldenburg Schloss, the castle, built in pleasing Baroque style. A short distance away stood the Neo-Gothic Lamberti Church, where I was singing in the annual *St. Matthew's Passion* as a soprano choir boy. To my left was my old school, now called "The Old Gymnasium," and the State Theatre, the place of Miss Nischewski's activity and the scene of my stagehand adventures. At the busy traffic corner, I passed Cafe Klinge, a favourite hangout of the afternoon coffee and cream Torte lovers (provided you had the money and the necessary food coupons.)

Next to the coffee shop, across from the fire hall, a meeting point of several highways and streets, a large conspicuous billboard caught my attention every day. As its inscription was in English, it was obviously not directed at the German population. It confused me, as it may have baffled the many Germans passing by:

"Ten Minutes with Venus, a Lifetime with Mercury."

Judging by the large dimensions of the sign and the prominence of its location, the cryptic nature of the message displayed, and the reference to the two planets, it must have been an important preconceived coded signal directed at the Canadian soldiers. I asked myself what the astral references to Venus and Mercury could mean. Why would the Canadian army invoke antique divinity? The average Canadian soldier was unlikely to be familiar with classical mythology. It was Private Henry Duval who solved the riddle. He had been briefed before leaving Aldershot and, although he could not explain the references to Venus and Mercury, he was aware that the advertising concerned *des maladies veneriennes*, sexually transmitted diseases. I recognized the symbolism, linking Venus as the goddess of love, legitimate or free, with the danger of contracting venereal diseases. As for the God Mercury, mercury, also called quicksilver, is the component of the notorious toxic grey ointment prescribed throughout the world by armies, friend or enemy alike, for the lifelong treatment of syphilis. The soldiers reading the sign had had their briefing and would be aware of the warning that at the same time was inoffensive to the civilian population. No doubt, it was a message from the astute Canadian Medical Officer at Division Headquarters, attempting to prevent or cut down on fraternization with the Oldenburg *frauleins*, to prevent his men from arriving home in Prince George, Trois Riviere, or New Glasgow with a dose of the clap, or worse.

Chapter 12

Except for food and clothes rationing, peacetime conditions returned gradually; life became normal again. When the universities re-opened, the students crammed the benches of institutes of higher learning, enforcing the introduction of the *numerus clausus*, the restriction of the number of admissions. I applied for matriculation in medicine and was accepted by the University of Göttingen. During the time of my first semester of premedical study, changes took place at the Oldenburg food office, the place of my recent employment. Colonel Gilbert was transferred to the town of Bonn where he was promoted to deal with the task of feeding the populous industrial Rhine-Ruhr district. Since Bonn is also a university town, I inquired about employment under the Colonel; his office replied that my post was available and suggested that I change from Göttingen to the Bonn University. The colonel's encouragement was not a result of my outstanding linguistic skills; hundreds of better-qualified competitors were vying for the position. It seemed that Colonel Gilbert preferred my *modus operandi* as an intermediary, an unofficial negotiator, rather than respond to rigid verbatim translation.

Bonn is an attractive traditional university town of easy-going carnival-celebrating wine-sipping Rhinelanders. Surrounded by pleasant hills and vineyards, its clement climate allows the growth of the mild German Riesling grape on the bank of the Rhine River. I grabbed hold of the opportunity and enrolled successfully at Bonn University for my subsequent semesters.

On the political scene, meanwhile, situating the parliament of the new German government, lead by Chancellor Konrad

Adenauer, posed a problem. As Berlin, the previous capital, now surrounded by the Russian-occupied zone, was difficult to access, the Federal German Republic established its seat in Bonn. The only prominent building available, a teachers' college, was altered to house the new parliamentary assembly. Soon, Colonel Gilbert's function expanded to include the American and the French zones of occupation and even my interpreter's activity extended to the federal level. However, since my choice of career was to become a medical doctor, I reduced my duties as head interpreter to important conferences between the German minister for Food and Agriculture and Colonel Gilbert and his team, cutting down on my working hours, my responsibilities, and my relative importance.

Classes at the university started early in the morning. Professor Siebke was the newly-appointed head of the faculty of Obstetrics and Gynecology, transferred to Bonn University from Hamburg, the port city on the Elbe River. In an immaculate white coat he stood there on the podium, delivering his initial lecture on injuries caused by precipitous childbirth, in particular the tears to the rectum and to the urinary bladder, their socially degrading consequences, and their prevention. To make certain that the audience was awake, his introductory words were: "Between Shit and Piss we are born." Reinforcing his Hamburg seaman's raw vernacular, the professor repeated the phrase; however, to soften its impact on academic decorum, he expressed the repetition in Latin: *"Inter faecem et urinam nascimur."* The young female student sitting next to me leaned over spontaneously and whispered: "I like the Latin version much better." I nodded agreement. I had not paid much attention to my bench neighbour and noted that she kept her dark brown hair short and was not unattractive with an interesting, intelligent face. The Professor's unorthodox introduction had upset me also, but Ursula and I would become used to Siebke's lecturing style as we got to know each other. The friendship lasted beyond our university years and led to our marrying. Her interest in obstetrics and devotion to maternal and child care continued; ultimately, during the next fifty years, she would attend to nearly two thousand live births, including Caesarean sections, not counting the call-outs for false labour.

Ursula's career in obstetrics resulted in her attending nearly two thousand live births.

Professor Siebke's syllabus exceeded the boundaries of obstetrics, crossing into the fields of human embryology, fetal legitimacy, and medical ethics. He kept us in suspense with his nearly science fiction topics when he discussed the eccentric subject of *superfoetatio.* "During the process of impregnation," he lectured, "as the human egg travels from the ovary to the uterus by way of the Fallopian tube, it is met halfway by a myriad of male sperm cells. As soon as one of them has penetrated the *zona pellucida*, a translucent layer surrounding the egg, all the other competing sperm cells of that ejaculate are rejected. Within a few hours, a protective membrane, the *decidua,* begins to form, which will cover, feed, and protect the fertilized ovum against further intrusion."

These were known facts of embryology; however, as Siebke explained, there are exceptions to this rule. "Assume that very shortly after the fist copulation, while the decidual cover is still incomplete, the woman is impregnated by a second male who is unrelated to the first. The fresh gush of sperm will proceed and confront the ovum. While the *zona pellucida* has become impervious to the first species of spermatozoa, there is no obstruction to the second, genetically different batch, as long as they can get past the rapidly closing blanket of the *decidua*. One of the flagellates will prevail, penetrate, and "super-fertilize" the egg. The fetus developing will now contain the genetic components of two different paternal sperm cells."

According to Siebke, an unfaithful woman, discovering in her offspring the characteristics from more than one father, might suspect the state of *superfoetatio*. Only she would be aware of the actual cause. Accordingly, evidence of the occurrence of *superfoetatio* would be anecdotal, depending on reports from the women. Siebke's research was restricted to identification through blood grouping only; chromosomal and DNA recognition of paternity were in the future. *Superfoetatio*, he said, would be more numerous in cases of promiscuous wives, in wartime during mass rapes, or in prostitutes. Although my experience of witnessing what went on in the beds on the school stage in the small village of Nachtigall re-emerged briefly in my memory, even to us students of medicine, *superfoetatio* was a confusing and embarrassing subject that we did not discuss among colleagues. What was the scientific evidence? Where was the proof? Academic discussion of *superfoetatio* seemed subjective, limited to keeping within the prevailing Zeitgeist. There was neither interest in nor money for scientific research in the results of polyandrous sex. However, the mystery was so intriguing that it did inspire me, when the time came for me to propose an original research topic, to focus on an area of embryology.

During medical classes, I had befriended Heinz Mevenkamp, another student and by now probably a retired radiologist. Hailing from Paderborn in Westphalia, Heinz was a good Catholic and had found his student's accommodation in a convent, the St. Agnes Stift (a denominational charitable institution), a residential school for delinquent girls, operated by Redemptorist nuns. The building, housing only females, was located on Römer Strasse, at the edge of the city, without protection. In those unstable post-war times, the Sisters were anxious to have an authoritative and reliable male living with them to prevent break-ins. On occasions when Heinz was away, he asked me to stand in for him, and the nuns were happy to have me living with them. Sister Berta was in charge of the comfortable and well-supplied apartment. I think she liked us; however, her rosy cheeks portended the high blood pressure, from which she died early. I have fond memories of the good Sister who took care of our earthly needs. Although Bonn was a predominantly Catholic region with occasional religious disputes, to the nuns of St. Agnes Stift, any source of protection was welcome, even if the protector's religious persuasion differed from theirs.

In keeping with Bonn's elevation to the new capital of Germany, changes took place at the food office that would affect me personally. A Canadian officer, Colonel Archibald Hugh McMillan, "Mister McMillan," as I called him, arrived and was appointed principal officer with the Control Commission for West Germany. His broad mandate included the responsibility for the residents of the Rhine and Ruhr Valley District. Born in Lethbridge, Alberta, in 1904, he would be joined shortly by his wife Louella, nee Brewster, and their three young boys. Colonel McMillan was promoted shortly to Senior Regional Officer and the McMillan family moved into a villa in Bad Godesberg on the Rhine River, just south of Bonn. His predecessor, my previous employer, Colonel Gilbert, was retiring and returned to England; however, the new Canadian colonel kept me on as his interpreter.

One day, the Colonel called me into his office for a private conference. He began by deploring the lack of organized schooling for the children of British personnel, including his three boys, and then asked me, would I be willing to look after the young McMillans--Hugh, Garry, and Robert--to teach, educate, and entertain them as best I could? I would move in and live with them in Bad Godesberg as a member of the family. The Colonel assured me that there would be no interfering with my studying medicine.

The generosity of his offer made me aware of how small a world I had lived in. I had never experienced such a magnanimity; the offer was an unheard-of opportunity. Except for the episodes when I took the place of my friend at the St. Agnes Stift, I had been restricted to marginal attic accommodation, a sleeping bag on an ex-military canvas folding cot, cooking my meals on a one-burner hotplate and, condoned by Sister Bertha, the occasional bath in the laundry room of the St. Agnes Stift, not to mention the still prevailing shortage of food for civilians. Such an offer to an ex-enemy who fought the Canadians on the Gothic Line a few years before, could only come from people of a different world, people who had a broader view of life.

Pete, the German driver of the Colonel's eight-cylinder Horch car, pulled up at the rooming house in Bonn and collected my shabby belongings, my books and clothes, to take to the McMillan's villa on Koblenzer Strasse in Bad Godesberg. I was shown to my room with white sheets and pillow cases on the bed, and that evening I had my first dinner with the family--the Colonel, his wife, the three boys, the chauffeur Pete, his wife Marlene, and the cook, Frau Laroche. We had roast beef with Yorkshire pudding and strawberry shortcake with whipped cream as dessert, all unusual novelties to a student accustomed to boiled potatoes and turnips. I was so excited during the meal, I hardly savoured the flavour of the meat and the difference between good dairy butter and cheap margarine.

After dinner, while the Colonel treated me to a small celebratory drink, I learned that he was a supporter of Alberta's Evangelist Premier Aberhart's Social Credit Party before the war. He reminisced that he was elected and served one term as a member of the legislature and had voted on a change of the province's liquor laws because of the too liberal selling and serving of alcohol. The motion was carried by the house and resulted in the absurd rule to lock the bar and prohibit the serving of liquor, beer, or wine on board commercial airplanes when crossing the provincial border, entering Alberta. The same restriction applied to passenger trains and buses. The new law turned out to be unpopular and cost MLA McMillan his seat in the legislature. He himself was not a teetotaler. Alcoholic drinks, although quite accessible, were not served routinely; I nevertheless acquired a taste for the unique flavour of the Canadian Schenley's "Golden Wedding" rye whisky, served in bubbling Seven-Up with a slice of fresh cucumber floating on top.

Organizing activities for the boys was exciting. They were bright children who enjoyed hiking along the shore of the Rhine; taking the ferry across to the Sieben Gebirge, the Seven Hills, where, according to folklore, Siegfried had slain the Dragon; learning and singing German wanderers' songs with them, some of which Hugh, Garry, and the youngest, Robert, remember to this day. Garry became a successful Broadway Thespian, Robert a civil servant of the Ministry of Social Affairs in Edmonton, and Hugh, the oldest with the authority of a first-born, the CEO of a trading company in Vancouver. I myself remember fondly the hours I spent with Colonel McMillan alone, especially when we were driving, and the fatherly counsel he offered me on subjects that I never imagined men discussed with other men. Even when we were on the road, the Colonel was exposing me to new experiences such as the exotic vegetable okra in the Chicken Gumbo soup he would inevitably order. He also had one favourite expression, which he repeated often--"benevolent dictator." I did not voice my suspicion that he identified personally with the concept.

The Colonel was never two-faced; he did everything out in the open even if it was painful to him or offensive to others. After a further promotion and added responsibilities, he moved his family into a palatial mansion near Coesfeld in Westphalia that had belonged to some high Nazi functionary such as a *Gau Leiter*, a position perhaps comparable to that of a governor of an American state. Located on a picturesque elevation, visible off the highway, the estate placed its occupants into a high social station. The McMillan family of five, the green keeper and his family who came with the property, as well as the driver and his wife, the housekeeper, the cook and her elderly husband who helped, and myself, the private tutor for the boys, all received accommodation and board in this complex beautifully appointed new home. To Louella McMillan's delight, the large living room contained a well-tuned grand piano, and all would have been harmonious and in good taste had not Archie, the Colonel, made a capital blunder.

From his residence, he sent Pete with the Horch car to Dortmund for Gertrud, his blonde German secretary, and spent some private hours with her in the master bedroom upstairs while his wife Lou sat on the couch downstairs in the living room, silent tears running down her face. I know; I sat next to her. The colonel had mentioned to me his plan a few days before. It was well-conceived, almost scientific, based on the use of the king-sized bed upstairs. In a circular motion, comparable to the hands on a clock face, the minute hand would go around; when the long hand covered the short one at the 12 o'clock configuration, he would climax. He described the manoeuvre as a personal experiment. In my mind, this was an unreasonable act, but I said nothing; it was too private.

At the time, Colonel McMillan was at the pinnacle of his power in a semi-military command over a large and populous area of Germany, the industrial Rhine-Ruhr District. With the almost unlimited means at his disposal, he must have felt a surge of power. Sending for the girl had nothing to do with libidinous sexual drive. It was a way to test his potential capacity, to see how far he could go in his eccentricity, to commit an act normally considered inconceivable, in complete disregard of conventional conduct. It was outside of his regular pattern of thinking and logic. I doubt if the boys were old enough to perceive what was going on In their home. In my mind, this was an unreasonable act of an otherwise reasonable and fine man of good character whom I knew intimately and from whom I adopted both good and bad habits such as flossing my teeth, smoking tailor-made Navy-Cut cigarettes, and spreading strawberry jam on top of the slice of cheese that covered the breakfast toast. In the same way that he ostentatiously expectorated from the car window when he himself was driving his luxury Horch convertible coupe, this was the Colonel's *modus operandi*, no deviousness, always above board, even if it inflicted pain.

That night, all family members, including the visiting Gertrud, were present at the dinner table. Louella McMillan was the perfect hostess who kept the painful matter to herself. It was not up to me to make postcoital inquiries; however, my thoughts drifted back to years before when Franz Spögler had me witness a telephone conversation between Mussolini's wife Rachele Mussolini and Claretta Petacci, the Duce's mistress, whose radio I had repaired. It did not require great knowledge of the Italian language to recognize the cataract of verbal abuse heaped upon the Duce's *amorosa*, conveyed via the official diplomatic German TF telephone channel. In contrast, Louella McMillan was a true lady. Despite occasional spats, of which the Colonel made no secret, I could sense harmony in a family where Louella was in charge of the house. She often enriched our evenings with her piano play and her alto voice, offering songs, mostly spiritual, such as William Blake's "Jerusalem." The lyrics are as exquisite as the melody is overwhelming:

And did those feet in ancient time walk upon England's mountains green? And was the Holy Lamb of God on England's pleasant pastures seen?
And did the countenance divine shine forth upon our clouded hills?
And was Jerusalem builded here among these dark satanic mills?

Despite his transgressions, this Canadian colonel had admirable qualities. At the dinner table, mostly for the benefit of the children, he plied us with funny stories and jokes. The boys were exhilarated by the one about a thief who steals a coat from a Winnipeg store and runs away down Portage Avenue. The Jewish owner summons the policeman: "Ossifer, ossifer! Shoot him in the pants; the coat is mine!" Another favourite was the tale of two little skunks named "In" and "Out" who one day get lost in the woods. When they fail to return for dinner, their mother goes looking for them. "In, Out, where are you? It's late!" Finally the mother skunk finds her two boys where they have been playing and herds them towards home. "Mommy, Mommy," the young one asks, "how did you find us?" "That's easy, darlings," replies their mother. "In stink(t)."

To better understand German mentality, Mr. McMillan had set his mind on learning German through my tutorship. There were many frustrating moments; he made many mistakes, some of which are even committed by Germans themselves, but he became fairly good at conversational German. His interest expanded when he asked about my university courses and the basic sciences, of which he had some knowledge. We were discussing biology and the capillary action of plants and trees. How do the sap, water, and nutrients ascend to the top of some trees over fifty metres tall? From his college years in a town called Edmonton he remembered one unusual theory and was able to quote an Indian scientist, Sir Jagadish Chandra Bose, who postulated that these tall trees go through certain slow electro-mechanical pulsations, a process of peristalsis, that pushes the fluid up. During my Basic Sciences term examination a few months later, the professor asked that very question and one of my answers was the Bose theory. It earned me top marks in that subject, and I did well in others, too, thanks to Colonel McMillan's Canadian education.

The Colonel was an active subscriber to the Book-of-the-Month Club, allowing me access to the works of John Dos Passos, Sinclair Lewis, Rachel Field, Upton Sinclair, Ernest Hemingway, Jack London, and whatever surprise the next overseas package might contain. His choices seemed to have a propensity toward socialism. It was all a new world to me with my one-party German upbringing.

The post-war occupation of Germany by the victorious allied powers ended officially on September 21, 1949 when the country's administration was returned into German civilian hands. The food branch of the British Control Commission disbanded, and the McMillans returned to Canada. It was the time of the atom bomb scare with public instructions on how to build your own private bomb shelter, and Archie, a private citizen now, wrote that he had obtained a position as the civil defence coordinator for the City of Edmonton.

Following their departure, I missed the personal closeness to this fine family. Mrs. McMillan, who seemed to have adopted me as her oldest and who sent numerous food parcels while I completed my studies, expressed her concern about my future. Finding suitable employment in a still-recovering Germany remained a challenge. The idea of emigrating to Canada moved more and more into the foreground. Three years after the McMillan's return to Canada, although not financially endowed, they sent me a money order to cover my fare to Canada. The envelope contained no request for an IOU or signed commitment, no mention of interest payments, just a short note: "We are doing this for you and for our country so that some day our contribution will make the world a better place to live in." My decision became obvious.

Chapter 13

It had taken five years to complete my studies and to graduate as a physician. However, to attain the title "Doctor of Medicine," it is necessary to show ability to perform independent research and to draw conclusions from the results. I had read about the empirical use of a new energy, called ultrasound, that had been introduced experimentally by the University of Bonn's dermatology department. Since its effect on internal organs was unknown, the use of ultrasound was restricted to treatment of superficial skin diseases, atopic dermatitis, psoriasis, and chronic eczema. As I had some knowledge in electronics and an interest in the field of embryology, piqued by professor Siebke's lectures on superfoetatio, I indicated my interest in researching the biological effect of ultrasound as a thesis topic for my doctorate. Professor Grütz, the *ordinarius* of the department, accepted my proposal and was able to obtain a government grant for the expenses of my project.

To research the effect of the new energy on organic tissue, I selected the most sensitive medium, live embryonic tissue, and started by collecting virginal frog eggs that I inseminated by pouring over them a suspension of ground-up frog testicles that I had liquefied in a mortar and pestle. I waited for the sign of early embryonic development when the one-cell frog egg multiplies into two, then four cells. At that stage, called the *blastula*, I exposed them to different doses and durations of ultrasound and observed the results. About seventy-five percent of the developing tadpoles exhibited deformities consistent with spina bifida, a malformation found also in human embryos and miscarriages, usually attributed to folic acid deficiency. The Journal for Radiation Therapy printed my findings, and I read the paper before a congress in Leipzig, resulting in the granting of the title of Doctor of Medicine. Since then, as a precaution, to reduce spina bifida formation, prenatal ultrasound scans are restricted to pregnancies beyond twenty weeks of age, after the human embryo's spinal canal is closed. The completion of the research gave me a lot of satisfaction since I had been permitted to do my work in total independence.

During my practical year that followed, I worked for a period of time as a *locum tenens*, a Latin term, which translates as "holding the place." Practicing physicians use the term to describe a temporary replacement during their absence from work for reasons of vacation, further study, or illness. As a locum, I free-lanced for regular doctors, doing house calls to administer strophantin injections to patients in heart failure. I knew of the drug's beneficial influence on the force of contraction of the heart muscle, called the positive inotropic effect. Strophantin's short half-life would preclude cumulative toxic effects. I also knew of another drug, digitalis, with similar properties. Although prescribing digitalis has considerable advantages over strophantin, except that its longer half-life can lead to toxic blood concentrations, it has a dangerously narrow therapeutic range. To start a patient on digitalis mandates careful blood level titration; an overdose is very toxic, and conversely, it is ineffective when the blood level is too low. This inconvenient attribute is outweighed by the drug's cheapness and the advantage of easy oral administration. Strophantin is known in Canada as Oubaine where its high cost and the cumbersome daily intravenous injections preclude its use in favour of digitalis, although the danger of intoxication is low due to its shorter half-life, hence the safer but cumbersome daily strophantin injections in the treatment of heart failure in Germany. In retrospect, one might wonder if strong lobbying by the strophantin producer played a role in the German preference of and adherence to that particular awkward heart failure medication. Another reason might well be the post-war lack of laboratory efficiency in assessing digitalis blood levels cheaply and consistently enough, considering the Nazi-inspired arrogant attitude of German researchers who doggedly continued to believe in the long-faded superiority of German scientists, finding themselves years behind the rest of the world. The intelligentsia had left Germany to benefit other nations.

The spirit of procrastination also prevailed at the place of my first employment after graduation. The post-war glut of available labour had followed students through their academic years and beyond graduation, including those pursuing the medical profession, and I was no exception. It was a buyers' market for hospitals seeking to obtain young assistant physicians. I jumped at the rare chance that was offered me, and, probably by virtue of my publication on ultrasound, I found employment as a resident intern in general medicine at the Weser Bergland Klinik, a privately-operated hospital in Höxter. By coincidence, in was in Höxter where the American Captain Beuer had signed my ticket to fredom.

The Weser Bergland Klinik in Höxter, erected after the war.

During the post-war years, Höxter had become the seat of a large, one hundred-bed private hospital. The Klinik claimed to be oriented toward new medical techniques and methods of treatment. In contrast to the conservative indications of the Bonn University that cautiously restricted its ultrasound application to the treatment of dermatological, surface disorders, the Weser Klinik took the bold step to apply ultrasound experimentally to patients with systemic chronic and incurable diseases such as Multiple Sclerosis (MS), Amyotrophic Lateral Sclerosis (ALS), becoming known in America as Lou Gehrig's disease after the well-known baseball player. The treatment list included intestinal disorders including Crohn's disease, osteoarthritis, even depression, and what is now referred to as Polymyalgia Rheumatica, as well as renal disorders. Without any double blind studies or concrete scientific evidence of efficacy, they might find almost any ailment an ultrasound-treatable disease.

In the hospital, I missed the presence of a library with access to recent scientific publications. I also resented the absence of the institution's teaching hospital status where young doctors could learn to apply the classical principles of diagnosis and therapy. Nor was it a place for treatment of acute diseases or for surgical procedures. Although the *Klinik* brazenly advertised the program of unorthodox and disputable new methods of ultrasound irradiation, it was rather a rehabilitation facility, REHA in German. The *Kranken Kasse*, the German health insurance carrier, assured payment of the cost of hospitalization and treatments for two weeks. The official head of the clinic was Professor Nonnenbruch, a physician of some political and scientific controversy, of which I did not learn until much later, after I had left Germany. The physician in charge of clinical medicine delegated me to the role of initiating other arrivals into the proceedings and routines of the large institution.

One of the clinic's two directors, Professor Lampert, had his mind set on an unusual therapeutic modality, colonic irrigation. The patient would be placed in a bath and receive, through the rectum, a continuous infusion of warm water to flush the colon; the return fluid was siphoned off, of course. The water temperature was kept at 38 degrees, ultimately raising the patient's body temperature to above normal. It was Lampert's theory that colonic irrigation would not only "clean out" the body's digestive tract, remove "toxins," at least from the terminal portion, the rectum, but the professor claimed, that the hyperthermia would effectively treat cancer and other chronic illnesses. In practice, however, there was no evidence that the water would even fill the entire length of the colon; it was only a rectal wash, comparable to a fancy enema. There were no double-blind studies; the treatment was evaluated solely by the patient's subjective report.

Lampert's second in command, Dr. Gross, researched the theory of the focal origin of disease, based on the assumption that a spurious, abnormal nervous pathway, either from chronic appendicitis, a chronic tooth abscess, or even lesser irritants such as an old scar, had brought on the patient's ailment. As a consequence, we, the assistants, were to search the body surface of every newly-admitted patient for scars, no matter how insignificant, and infiltrate the surrounding tissue with one percent Novocain, applying blocks to the assumed faulty nerve impulses. We were to observe the effect, watching for a break in the imputed vicious circle by subsequent improvement in the patient's complaint, either in the form of less pain or, in the case of paralysis, the return of function. I have no recollection of positive results of either Lampert's colonic irrigation or of Gross' Novocaine injection trials, nor does any medical paper confirm a favourable outcome of these pursuits.

The third person in the clinic's triumvirate of scientific pinnacles, Professor Wilhelm Nonnenbruch, was respected by us young doctors as a scientist of great esteem and sophistication for his participation in the research on the so-called Goldblatt Kidney. A Dr. Goldblatt had published that blocking kidney circulation causes a rise in blood pressure through the release of the hormone Renin. This discovery initially received great interest in the research on the origin of hypertension, which, however, is now known to have other, more prominent causes than the less frequent interference with renal circulation. Still, Professor Nonnenbruch was said to be the exalted grand master of German medicine although, during my time under him, he was recovering from a disabling stroke. He seems to have served more as a figurehead by the merit of his past scientific achievements, we young assistants assumed.

While I was working at the Höxter klinik, some distance from home, my friend Ursula was completing her medical internship at a Bonn hospital, and to save her the inconvenient visits by hitch-hiking the considerable distance to Höxter, I had purchased a small 100 cc motor bicycle. Since the restoration of the German government's authority, the disbandment of the British food administration, and Colonel McMillan's return to Canada, my two income sources, interpreter and tutor, had vanished. Except for the paltry doctor's salary from the Klinik, I was penniless and spent my spare time reading and interpreting electrocardiograms at the fee of three marks per tracing. This additional income served to pay off the loan from Mother for the motor bike. Although my activity at the Weser Clinic was not challenging, a new position would be difficult to find. For every vacancy there was an abundance of medical applicants. My professional future did not seem rosy. At that moment in time, a letter arrived from the McMillans who had moved to New Westminster, British Columbia, containing a $240 money order, the cost of a single fare by ship and rail to as far as Winnipeg, Canada. Ursula and I decided to take the step together. She arranged for and obtained a monetary sponsorship from a distant relative, Mr. Michael Dumont, a prominent Vancouverite, who advanced her fee, including the cost of her initial stay at the Winnipeg YWCA.

Ursula, interning at a Bonn hospital, was visiting when I was working at the Weser Clinic.

The heads of the *Klinik* had learned of my plan to immigrate to Canada and, shortly before my departure, Professor Nonnenbruch called me in. "I hear you are leaving us, Doctor Asche. While I was teaching at the German University in Prague (after the forceful annexation and German occupation of Czechoslovakia), I had a very gifted student who is now Professor at the University of Montreal. He is famous for his research on adaptation and the stress syndrome that is associated with the newly-discovered drug cortisone. I have written an introduction for you to Professor Selye; I have asked him to help you become established in Canada." The good doctor, as if the letter contained a direct order to assist me by the strength of his assumed previous authority, handed me the important envelope and bade me good-bye with the patronizing admonition: "You must visit my previous pupil, Professor Selye!" His voice became hoarse and he had tears in his eyes, because the stroke had caused an imbalance of his vaso-motor system that made his eyes water on such occasions.

Ursula and I settled our affairs in Germany and obtained from the police the required certificates of good conduct. Restricted by the funds available, crossing the Atlantic via luxurious, more expensive, and perhaps more risky air travel was not our choice. We embarked on the SS Seven Seas out of Bremerhaven as steerage passengers, and the ship took on more immigrants in Le Havre and Liverpool. We slept in bunk beds with clean sheets, and the food was good. The old ark took her time; after ten days of shuffleboard and the odd bout of sea sickness, we arrived in Montréal on June 23, 1952, my birthday. The coincidence reminded me of some of my previous birthdays, in 1938 my pre-war bike visit to Holland and my reluctant participation in the military invasion of other countries such as Lithuania in 1940 and Italy in 1942. It was on my thirty-second birthday when I stepped on Canadian soil, this time, however, not as an enemy invader but peacefully, with the new country's permission and a letter of introduction. When our ship moored at the King Edward Quay in Montreal, now a quiet, historic site, the giant docks were swarming with immigrants--DPs (displaced persons) from Germany, Poland, Hungary, Czechoslovakia and the Ukraine, augmented by French and Irish.

After clearing immigration and customs, empty hours before the train's scheduled departure west allowed time for the important mission--to visit Professor Selye at the University of Montreal. He was friendly, spoke to us gracefully in German, and acknowledged the greetings from the Old Country. As we mentioned the name Nonnenbruch, however, he seemed to retreat, appearing preoccupied and very busy, and we could not help noting the rising coolness in his response as I handed him the reference letter. He took it and placed it unopened on the far corner of his desk. Soon we said good-bye to the Canadian scientist and were on our way again. Our duty call completed to a somewhat less than warm reception, we did not realize that the closed door of Professor Selye's office signalled the past we had left behind, the old world of a Nazi-ravaged Europe. When we boarded the westbound train, anticipating days of travel through the land which would become our new home, we saw ice blocks loaded into the kitchen and dining cars and realized the enormous distance to travel. It was the time before electric refrigeration on the train, and the steam locomotive was pulling us forward into the future—to Winnipeg at least, which was as far as Colonel McMillan's loan carried us.

Throughout the ensuing years in Canada, I duly kept Nonnenbruch's image in respect and veneration, trying to fathom Professor Selye's lukewarm brush-off instead of the expected welcome on behalf of his old teacher. It was only quite recently, when available information revealed Nonnenbruch's less glorious medical and political past, that I learned what had been well known to the rest of the world, including Professor Selye, but had been kept from our knowledge within Germany. The respected specialist for metabolic and renal diseases was a previous member of the SA and Obersturmbannführer in the SS. While in the German-annexed Czechoslovakia, he had become leader of the Nazi doctors' association, propagating their political ideas instead of medical knowledge. One of his students was the notorious concentration camp doctor Rudolf Brachtel, whom he taught to perform liver needle biopsies, a technique he later applied in his KZ practice, albeit without anaesthesia. As an SS officer Nonnenbruch had attended meetings held by the armaments ministry discussing the use of the plastics by-product Mycel as ersatz food for concentration camp inmates. From 1944 on he was advisor to Karl Brandt, head of the Nazi health system. And since 1940, he had been a member of the German Nazi Academy of Nature Research, a pseudo-scientific movement.

Professor Hans Selye was a genius in his own right. The results of his research, such as the effect of cortisone, initially called Compound E, on stress, while interesting and remarkable, are based on discoveries of others before him; they did not change medical treatment or improve therapy. Selye coined a new name, Stress, for something that was known already. Unlike the Canadian discoverers of Insulin, Banting and Best, Professor Selye, although nominated numerous times, fell short of reaching the Pantheon of science, the Nobel Prize.

Embarking on the *Seven Seas.*

Gerd Asche

Printed in Canada